What We Keep

Advice from Artists and Designers on Living with the Things You Love

Jean Lin

Abrams, New York

For Ma and Ba who gave me everything and taught me to treasure the beauty within.

Foreword	6
Introduction	8
Colony	10

Wood

Profile: Adam Rolston	20
How to Mix Wood in a Room	26
Studio: KWH Furniture	28
Studio: Grain Design	34
How to Identify Wood	40
Profile: Brent Buck	42
Studio: Mira Nakashima, in Her Words	48

Fire

Profile: Speaklow	60
How to Tame Fire	64
Studio: Deborah Czeresko	66
Profile: Preeti Sriratana	70
Studio: Stephanie H. Shih	76
Studio: MKCA	80

Earth

Profile: Sri Threads	90
How to Understand Textiles Online	96
Studio: Hiroko Takeda	98
How to Collect Brushes	104
Studio: M. Callahan	106
How to Bare It All	112
Profile: Two Tastemakers Tell All	114
Profile: Leyden Lewis	118
Profile: Jonathan Boyd	122
Profile: Animal Kingdom	126
How to Collect Body Parts (a Guide)	132
Profile: Maya Schindler	134

Metal

Studio: Robert Highsmith   144
How to Collect Sterling Silver   150
    (For Beginners Like Me)
Profile: Collecting Auböcks   152
Profile: Allyson Rees and Julius Metoyer   156
How to Collect Dunnies   164

Water

Profile: Worrell Yeung   172
Profile: A Kitchen Collection   176
How to Find the Flow   178
Profile: Aleishall Girard Maxon   180
Profile: Carlos Runcie Tanaka and   188
    James Tanaka
How to Share a Space   192
Profile: Phillip Collins, Good Black Art   194

Before You Go   202
Acknowledgments   204
About the Author   205
Contributors   206
Photography Credits   208

Foreword

When I first met Jean seven years ago at Colony, the cooperative for independent makers she founded in New York City, one of the things we immediately bonded over was our shared love of the "why" in home design. Don't get me wrong; we are "what" people, too, impressed by the labor and skill that goes into the kinds of patchwork quilts, walnut sideboards, and sculptural upholstered seating Colony puts on view. But our mutual appreciation for the emotional resonance things have, and why people choose to live with them, is what got me excited to know more about Jean's work.

1   Colony is a design gallery that represents independent American designers that celebrates both the "what" and the "why" of design.

What follows in these pages is an exploration of dozens of "whys," and a look at fascinating collections of objects of every kind.

What follows in these pages is an exploration of dozens of "whys," and a look at fascinating collections of objects of every kind, deployed with style and thoughtfulness in the homes of architects, artists, editors, and so many more. The items in question are all precious, but not pretentious. Across the collections, there are stories of family, curiosity, perseverance, and no small dose of (healthy) obsession. If while reading this you have an experience like mine, you'll start to look at the objects in your life with new eyes.

—Asad Syrkett
Editor in chief, **ELLE** Decor

Introduction

As we move through life, deciding on what we keep is, for many of us, the nascency of understanding the true value of the objects within our homes. This ritual turns a curiosity into an obsession, a hobby into an art, and a singular object into a collection.

1   Collections are so much more than simply things, as what we choose to keep, over time, becomes a reflection of who we are.

At its most magical, design is beautiful, meaningful, and lasting. Not simply about an object, a room, or any one item, the magic lies in the interaction that we have with it, the space between. Design exists in the lives of the people who love collecting items over time for reasons utilitarian, political, emotional, nostalgic, fiscal, and highly personal. These collections are often reflections of people's lives. These pieces and the places they inhabit can reveal something of who we are—as creative professionals, as neighbors, as friends, as mothers and daughters, as contributors to a society—a place in history that we can be proud of.

This book posits that beauty of an object is that of substance, a physical representation of the people who create, use, trade, and collect it. The Five Elements are our five sections, each encapsulating a chapter that recalls a unifying style, process, trait, mindset. Each chapter describes both design and people, all sharing in a pursuit of purpose and balance in their homes, their art, and, ultimately, their lives.

—Jean Lin, 2023

Colony

[1] Colony is a cooperative design gallery where independent American designers find support and community.

I met my college boyfriend at a record store. Rather, I saw him at the record store where he worked, and I proceeded to stalk him for months, laying stacks of obscure CDs I definitely couldn't afford on the checkout counter in an effort to impress him with my extensive knowledge of music. This story, however, is not about Mike, who called me a half hour after I finally gave him my number; it's about his sister Katie.

Katie was an artist in the truest sense of the word who lived in Vermont with her boyfriend, Josh, and their baby, Gus. They shared a log cabin in the middle of, according to my keen navigational observations: nowhere. But the cabin was warm and quirky, a visual catalog of Katie and Josh's passion for art and music. Katie's paintings hung on the walls, sculptures made of macabre found objects (bones, feathers, teeth?) lined the windowsills, and homemade musical instruments entertained Gus for hours. I can't remember their furniture; I'm sure it was humble, not only because they weren't wealthy, but mainly because they treasured objects in a different way than that. So much that they had was beautiful, but mostly in the sense that each piece slyly revealed a little more about who they were as individuals and as a family.

It was with Katie, Josh, Gus, and Mike that I first fell in love with vintage thrifting.

It was with Katie, Josh, Gus, and Mike that I first fell in love with vintage thrifting. We met on weekends in a small New England town on the border of Vermont and Massachusetts and spent hours digging through what can only be described as trash, to uncover the perfect—trash. Haggling was thrilling, and I would gingerly shuttle home my newest—trash—wrapped in layers of gray newsprint and triumphantly place it on my own windowsill, imagining someday in the unnamed future when I would reveal my heart in my home as beautifully and genuinely as Katie did.

Many more apartments, three college degrees, two cities, and an adopted puppy named Bosco later, Mike and I broke up. Earlier that year, I was lying in my mom's bed, chatting, feet propped up on her dark wood headboard, excitedly announcing that it was my year. I was twenty-four, and it was the Year of the Rooster, my Chinese zodiac sign. My mother was suspiciously quiet, and, at the end of that year—after the breakup, after losing my job and having to take on several part-time gigs to make ends meet—I sighed, ". . . but it was my year."

"I didn't want to tell you, you were so excited," she said in her half-Chinese, half-English cadence that me and my brothers delight in. Apparently, Chinese superstition says that every twelve years, when your birth year Zodiac sign comes around, you are cursed with bad luck. I write this with absolutely zero authority, and, in fact, my mother's version of the superstition is an elaborately fuzzy, certainly fabricated fable that involves the animals of the zodiac . . . offending one another? Or something?

It is on the same shaky authority that I share that I am a Metal Rooster, born in 1981. This means that I am diligent and persuasive and optimistic and pragmatic and attractive. Each year is assigned an animal *and* an element—did you know? I did not. But as an adult, a gallery owner and a designer, the Five Elements are ever relevant. The elements—Wood, Fire, Earth, Metal, and Water—provide a theoretical foundation that applies to all facets of traditional Chinese thinking. (Yes, astrology, but also feng shui, the martial arts, and traditional Eastern medicine.) These elements, never static, are also rooted in their relationships to one another:

> Wood feeds Fire, Fire makes Earth, Earth creates Metal, Metal holds Water, and Water nourishes Wood.
> Wood roots Earth, Earth dams Water, Water extinguishes Fire, Fire melts Metal, and Metal cuts Wood.

These relationships dictate balance in all the natural world, including within ourselves, our work, and our personalities. The elements affect us in ways both obvious and discreet, such as when they guided me on a winding path to the beginning of my business.

It was Halloween 2012. I didn't have a costume planned that year, but no matter, because Hurricane Sandy had barreled through New York City in the days prior and decimated life as we knew it. They called it "Superstorm Sandy," a name that made me scoff. Wasn't there a marketing team that could have come up with something a little less—on the nose? But giggles were hushed in shame and gave way to dread when we walked outside and observed the destruction firsthand. If you aren't sold on the power of the Five Elements of nature, simply walk through the aftermath of a natural disaster such as Sandy in a city such as mine. Water and Wind had felled Wood, moved Earth, and corrupted Metal, leaving downtown Manhattan in the dark for days after a devastating electrical Fire and explosion.

The split and fallen trees, languidly draped over cars and power lines, inspired an idea. Where just days before stood trees, we now saw piles and piles of wood. My friend Jen and I frantically planned and

INTRODUCTION

produced Reclaim NYC, a design exhibit of work made out of debris from the storm and sold for storm relief. We invited independent designers, artists, and makers to participate—and they accepted, donating their time, their talent, and their resources to the show. They were all New Yorkers who shared in the horror of what we were facing as a city, with a particular harrowed urgency for the underprivileged facing the oncoming winter with no respite from the lasting water damage, failed public transit, and fried power grid.

Also born from this show were countless dinners, studio visits, and friendships. From Reclaim NYC I grew a deeper understanding of these independent makers, designers, and artists. They are small business owners who are also master craftspeople, creating lasting, meaningful, and ultimately functional works of art and design that I now showcase and sell at my cooperative gallery Colony, located in the same Downtown Manhattan neighborhood that sat in the dark for weeks after the hurricane.

Reclaim NYC gave me the courage to believe I could run a successful business grounded in the strength of community and the power of relationships, a business that values the greater good as much as its bottom line. Like a dream come true, Colony is also a business that allows no compromise of my understanding of meaningful, lasting, and real beauty. This understanding has grown from the metaphorical seedlings planted at Katie's house in the woods of Vermont, has matured through my education in fashion design at Parsons School of Design in New York City, and is actualized within the interiors of homes around the world through my work at Colony. I do design homes as a self-taught interior designer, but more often I admire the work of my clients at Colony, a growing stable of wildly talented interior designers who come to see the pieces and support the studios of those craftspeople I fell in love with after the storm. It's this work, by these interior designers, and by this community of independent makers, that populates the pages of this book.

Wood

Begin at the beginning, they say. And when speaking of the home, there is no better place to start than wood. It is foundational in our built environment. Buildings, furniture, objects, paper can all be reduced to wood.

1

1   The hand-carved ash wood Cove/Arc Credenza by KWH Furniture sits below the Lummi quilt by Meg Callahan.

P. 14   Slabs of wood wait to become masterpieces in the Nakashima Woodworkers lumber sheds.

P. 15   Handmade equestrian dental tools from Brent Buck's collection.

P. 16   A sculptural wood floor lamp by Michael Gilmartin, from Adam Rolston's vintage collection.

P. 17   Grain Design's Dish coffee table (in ash) sits next to Vonnegut/Kraft's oak Relevé Dining Table at Colony.

(See page 206 for additional information.)

So many of us have memories of loudly upturning a bucket of wood blocks onto the living room carpet, learning scales on an upright piano, carving our initials into a tree in the yard, recoiling from a splinter as a result, or finding the perfect Y-shaped branch to make a slingshot. It's no wonder that wood is so ingrained in our sense memories that it is a core element in the broadest of human experiences.

Aspiring furniture makers, too, will likely begin with the wood that's readily available from a local hardware store. They chip and whittle and saw and glue and sand their way to their masterpieces. Nary is there an interior designer or architect who doesn't love wood. Transcending stylistic tastes and eras, wood furnishings, floors, walls, and details are ubiquitous in almost any home, making it both essential and specific to the design world.

Adaptable and hardworking, the wood element's personality is one of many facets: grounded and visionary, historical and lasting, hard and soft, but above all evergreen in relevance.

IN THIS SECTION:

20   An architect finds meaning in empty boxes.
26   Mixing wood with confidence.
28   KWH Furniture
34   A lesson in FSC and sustainable wood.
40   Know the different species of wood.
42   See every mid-century Dansk pepper mill ever produced.
48   Mira Nakashima reconciles her personal history and her father's legacy.

Profile: Adam Rolston

1

1. WOOD
20

1   Adam and Martin's home is filled with art traded with friends, greenery, and collections that are close to their hearts.

Stories that start with "Back in the ACT UP days . . ." intrigue me and hint at a man that I only thought I knew. Adam Rolston is a founding partner at INC, the architecture and design studio responsible for many iconic New York City spaces such as the renovated Rockefeller Center and the TWA Hotel. But digging into his history, it's clear that Adam is much more than the architect: He is the son, the partner, the brother, the father, the friend, the business partner, the boss, the artist, the gay rights activist.

Adam and his partner Martin's home is a living workshop showcasing Adam's creative drive and Martin's scientific wonderment (Martin is a research psychologist). Glass beakers sit on a cabinet in front of a painting of a man looking suspiciously like Adam, dressed partially in drag.

"The art is mine or otherwise bartered and traded over the years," says Adam with not the slightest hint of nostalgia. "We arrived in New York in the eighties, and the AIDS epidemic was already here. Our work with ACT UP was intertwined with our art. It was unavoidable and it was one in the same." Items of intrigue abound, starting with the art and continuing to the furnishings—including a towering Seussian wood floor lamp. "I bought that lamp when we were working on the lobby of a building that was exploring amorphous forms in architecture," he explains, showing rather than telling how his home and his work are one in the same—for Adam, design is an all-encompassing activity.

> **I asked Adam and Martin if they collected anything, and they looked at each other sheepishly, explaining they had a lot of stuff but weren't collectors.**

Before I ever saw their apartment, I asked Adam and Martin if they collected anything, and they looked at each other sheepishly, explaining they had a lot of stuff but weren't collectors. Then Adam nodded at Martin and said, "Boxes." Both looked at their toes, as if they were embarrassed to call it a collection, or that the collecting had been unintentional, that one morning they had simply awakened to a pile of boxes. But in fact, the collection of boxes that Martin and Adam share—mainly wood, varying in shape, displayed and stacked with care— is thoughtful and considered.

"The boxes are Martin's thing," Adam declares boldly; then he pauses and redacts. "Well, conceptually they connect to both of us." He continues to reflect on the collection in a stream-of-consciousness way:

> "There is never anything in them.
> "The boxes are all empty.
> "They represent utility.
> "Or the beauty in a *lack* of utility.
> "Or the option for utility.
> "We *could* put something in them. The option is there.
> "They represent potential."

2   Glass, marble, wood, and metal coexist in harmony when each element is thoughtfully applied.

3   Adam and Martin display their vintage boxes in tapered stacks. This creates a sense of order and highlights how varied the collection really is.

4   Artwork is hung on cable rails along every wall in Adam's home; the verticality of the method is offset by a continuous horizontal break in color. The colors change from room to room, but the height of the break is consistent throughout the apartment.

COLLECTED THOUGHTS

Adam's history and future are both tied to his collections; they are a physical representation of the emotional importance he places on art, design, and his sense of home.

1. WOOD

2

3

4

5

5   An iron work sculpture and a photographic print by Randy Gibson from his *Available Light Symmetry* series give Adam and Martin's collection of vintage boxes a contemporary luster.
6   Vintage clocks hang as decor, not one still works. The display creates a sense of nostalgia for analog and an old-time futurism, where time travel is tracked by gears and knobs.

How to Mix Wood in a Room

So many of our friends and clients are reticent and confused about mixing wood species in the same room or house. "Can we have dark wood chairs with all that light wood in the kitchen?" Though it might seem counterintuitive, mixing woods is essential to creating a textured, warm, and lived-in room.

PICK FAVORITES
Rank your favorite species based on color, grain, and feel. If you love walnut, let that dictate the larger pieces in the room, dotting lighter woods through smaller items and accessories.

THE POWER OF THREE
Try to have at least three different tones of wood in the room. One is too matchy-matchy, two is too contrasty, three is just right.

IRL IS KING
Please don't buy an investment piece without seeing it in person first. You can bring small things from your room (a throw cushion, a box, a tray) to the store to see it with your own eyes. Most independent makers and some larger retailers offer free material samples, so you can also request a swatch, take it home, and see if the tone of wood is right for your room before you buy.

WHEN IN DOUBT, ADD BLACK
This may be a little controversial, but a pop of black looks good almost anywhere. If you are worried one wood or another isn't going to go with something in your room, see if that item is available in a black lacquered, painted, or stained wood. Black never lets us down.

---

1   Choosing a single accent color, like the red tones seen here, makes the mixture of wood tones in the room a neutral, yet textured backdrop.

2   This dining table mixes walnut and ash, playing up contrasts. A walnut dining bench completes this eclectic palette.

3   Patina and age unify this collection of vintage chairs and furniture. Different species and tones of wood in the furnishings are like different chapters of the same story.

1

2

3

Studio: KWH Furniture

1

1. WOOD

1   KWH Furniture's wood studio in the Brooklyn Navy Yard proves that organization is a key component to precision in design.

Designer and woodworker Kai-wei Hsu was sitting on Colony's painted-white floor, sorting and organizing our toolbox. He had pulled it out of the closet, looking for a screwdriver, and couldn't stomach my haphazard disorganization: screws, pencils, hooks, and wires jangling loose in the bottom of my "toolbox," a cute canvas tote with boxy outer pockets. (Not necessarily the most practical thing for our tools, but adorable.) He patiently sorted and categorized everything, then quietly shook his head when, a month later, he stopped by and noticed it was all in disarray again.

One visit to his woodshop, KWH Furniture, puts it all in perspective. His work, crafting wood furniture, is intricate and laborious at once. A messy shop could spell disaster for the mindset he needs to machine massive solid wood boards into smooth, curved, and precise designs.

His interest in fine wood furniture started where so many great things start: with an ex. "My high school girlfriend's mom owned a gallery that represented studio furniture, so their home was filled with amazing furniture made from the same crazy wood as the guitars I was obsessed with—I thought it was so cool. So, when I was going into my sophomore year at RISD [Rhode Island School of Design] and the furniture department was established, I thought it was fate." Kai-wei's professors in school were the very makers he had admired at his ex-girlfriend's house, and they confirmed that her mom, Judy Coady, was instrumental in supporting their careers as young furniture designers.

Kai-wei's work now reflects years of perfecting his craft and understanding the material. He had a stint working for luxury interior architect Peter Marino and spent a longer time working for an aspiring furniture maker whose primary business was building outdoor decking. "Robert Martin was my mentor, [and] he made beautiful furniture, but we would mainly work with lumber for decks. He taught me what I know, but the outdoor installation of decking was rough, and I knew on-site work wasn't what I wanted for my own practice." It's with reverence for Robert's mentorship that Kai-wei shares, "He developed dementia and eventually had to stop working. I purchased the tools in this shop from his widow and inherited the lease on the space."

2   Kai-wei Hsu of KWH Furniture stands among his lumber collection.

"I've started to let the material and the process speak in the design itself."

The shop is immaculate. Yes, out of utility, but also out of respect. Respect for the art of woodworking, the tools that make it possible, and the history of the room where Kai-wei honed his skill. And isn't there such poetry in that? Robert's mentee is now making fine furniture in the very shop where together they once hauled around lumber, employing the woodworking mastery he learned from laying decks with Robert. "When I started designing my own furniture, I was drawn to more decorative concepts, like creating patterns out of veneer and using really nice hardware," Kai-wei admits, "because for so long, I was working with just lumber." But in recent years he's returned to solid wood as informative and pivotal to his work. "I've started to let the material and the process speak in the design itself."

COLLECTED THOUGHTS

An heirloom, such as a piece of handcrafted furniture, represents not only its maker but also the mentors and teachers who guided them along the way. As the person using and cherishing it, you are a crucial part of this beautiful lineage.

1. WOOD

3   Plywood and veneer in the shop

4–5 Kai-wei's work reflects years of perfecting his craft and understanding the tools and materials.

1. WOOD

4

5

Studio: Grain Design

1. WOOD

1 Furniture studio Grain Design's founding ethos is to make furniture that cherishes our planet, including this cork table. Cork is made from the bark of its tree, carefully harvested to keep the tree alive as a renewable resource.

"What's your favorite color?"

It's a question we are faced with often as designers. I never really know how to answer it, because I have such an appreciation for so many colors, each one evoking a different mood, memory, or feeling. It's almost impossible to pick one. But if I really consider the truth, I know the answer was there before I became a designer, long before I understood color on an intellectual level, experiencing it in a purely visual and emotional way.

I grew up in central Massachusetts, a sleepy New England town that for two to four weeks of every year was lit ablaze with color. Sometime in early October, the trees reached their peak. The red, orange, and yellow foliage was vibrant, fluorescent, and all-encompassing. Autumn in New England is my favorite color. Sometimes, on a gray, rain-laden fall day in New York City, I can close my eyes and still see the effervescent, golden glow that the trees bestowed upon us back home year after year.

I remember the first time I thought it. *The leaves aren't as bright, the color is dulled this year.* We blamed it on a rainy summer, an early frost, or happenstance, but every succeeding year has proven the sad reality that our planet has changed, as have my colors of autumn. All that remains are my childhood memories of leaves so bright they burned past physical recognition and settled in a sixth sense that existed between stupor and elation.

The New England trees that raised me into a designer, the now-beetle-infested forests of dying ash, and the old-growth teak that supplied the mid-century modern movement at the ultimate cost—just three examples of how precious a commodity wood really is. When faced with the loss of something so precious, the best we can do is to educate ourselves and find ways to contribute to solutions, rather than accepting the status quo. And with wood products, it's all about the trees.

FSC, or the Forest Stewardship Council, certification may sound familiar. It graces many commercial wood products as a stamp of eco-friendly approval and traces the origins of a product to the forest where its wood was harvested. The FSC certification is a tool for companies and consumers to ensure that their wood products did not come from an ecologically destructive process. The guilty parties of the international timber trade historically—and currently—profit from clear-cutting rainforests (so there's no chance for regrowth), destroying land populated with Indigenous people, and destroying waterways among other harms. FSC certification is an accountability check for lumber companies to avoid these practices.

"FSC is a good tool, but not a perfect one," says James Minola. James and his wife, Chelsea, are the pair behind Grain Design, a furniture, lighting, and textile studio based on Bainbridge Island, Washington, and they have dedicated their entire adult lives to promoting sustainable practices in design. "There is wood that you can't really get FSC[-certified], because that's a forest certification. There are some species that aren't grown in that way. The easiest domestic example is walnut. It's not often that you can get FSC[-certified] walnut, because it doesn't grow in a forest setting. Walnut trees are often off on their own somewhere, and forest management doesn't apply there."

How do Chelsea and James navigate a business called *Grain*—yes, as in wood grain—and their commitment to sustainability? It's hard. First, they buy only domestic wood for their designs. James notes, "It circumvents so many factors we can't control, like justice issues and the carbon footprint of importing lumber." Next, they work primarily with ash, a species that is farmed specifically for lumber use. One silver lining to the sad, inevitable extinction of ash is that the wood Grain Design uses is largely already dead, meaning they can avoid participating in cutting down live trees.

That is, until ash runs out.

Which is why James and Chelsea have been developing works made from cork. Cork is harvested from the bark of certain evergreen oaks, leaving the trees alive and rapidly able to grow more bark. Working with cork is only one of many ways Chelsea and James are looking to the future with hope.

2   When asked for tips on how to live (and collect) more sustainably, Chelsea says the easiest thing to do is shop local and acquire vintage and antique furniture, as seen here mixed with their own designs.

"Something we're slowly moving into is working directly with urban salvage lumber for trees that cannot be FSC certified, like walnut," James explains. "Urban salvage is a practice of milling lumber out of trees that are coming down for [land] development, or overgrowth in cities, or other reasons. This is forest-free lumber, and working directly with lumber mills that practice urban salvage gives us the opportunity to know the exact chain of custody our wood has been through."

Chelsea adds, "It's a spiritual relationship, working with a living thing like a tree. You feel it. You can see its growth marks, and you start to understand the relationship it has with our own bodies and with our world. To me, working with wood is a spiritual practice, and it takes a lot of reverence."

Companies like Grain Design give us a cheat sheet on how to make ecologically responsible purchases and acquisitions. Finding local small businesses that work with domestic wood species is a significant step toward creating a more ecologically friendly home. Choosing items that we love and that are built to last generations is another real step in the right direction. And wood itself ain't so bad, either.

"We're starting to see forward-thinking architects designing cutting-edge, large-scale buildings built entirely of timber," says James optimistically. "They've found that it's much more sustainable than steel or concrete. So, of the material options we currently have, wood is one of the most sustainable if it's done in the right way."

3   Stacks of ash lumber at Grain Design. Ash is becoming extinct because of an invasive beetle, but Chelsea and James prefer using it (by harvesting trees that have died) to minimize cutting down live trees for their furniture.

4   Inspiration at Grain Design

COLLECTED THOUGHTS

Companies like Grain give us a cheat sheet on how to make ecologically responsible purchases and acquisitions:

- *Find local, small businesses that work with domestic wood species.*
- *For a more sustainable home, choose items you love (and that are built to last generations.)*
- *And wood itself ain't so bad, either.*

3

4

How to Identify Wood

The categorizations for wood are twofold: domestic vs. exotic and hardwood vs. softwood. When thinking about the scale, cost, and carbon expenditure to ship lumber overseas, you start to understand why the domestic vs. exotic categorization is such an important one. Since I am in the United States, I'll categorize North American species as domestic.

Hardwood is made from deciduous trees, the ones that lose their leaves in the fall. Softwood comes from conifers, also known as evergreen trees. The difference? Hardwoods are generally more versatile, more expensive, and have a wider range of colors. While most species of hardwood are *usually* physically harder than softwoods, this is not always the case, making the nomenclature both misleading and somewhat confusing.

1 Oak cabinets, floors, and island create a monochromatic kitchen. Oak is a workhorse that allows for other materials, like the marble backsplash and counter, to shine.

1. WOOD

OAK
Domestic, Hardwood

Oak is the friend you've had since elementary school; you know her and you love her. I would describe the typical color of oak as toasted wheat. A rich light brown. Depending on the cut of the lumber, the grain can be swirly rivers or linear, thin flakes. Oak is a favorite with furniture makers, and most of the time, if wood isn't too light or too dark, it's oak.

WALNUT
Domestic, Hardwood

Walnut is the fancy girl you're dating but not sure you deserve. Its color is deep, warm brown, the color of hazelnut spread. There are all sorts of crazy grain patterns you can find in walnut, but the most common is a tight, smooth, tonal grain. Walnut furnishings are often accented with the rich golden hues of brass, a timelessly beautiful pair.

ASH, MAPLE
Domestic, Hardwood

Ash and maple are the twins who swear they aren't identical, but you have your doubts. Both are very light, almost white, but maple is lighter, and ash is a little yellow. Maple has a softer grain, while ash has a distinct, almost psychedelic grain. Many designers use bleached ash or maple for a white finish that foregoes paint and retains the beauty of wood. Ash is going extinct, thanks to a nationwide infestation of the emerald ash borer, an invasive beetle originating in Asia and decimating the North American ash population.

DOUGLAS FIR
Domestic, Softwood

Douglas fir is the softwood that is most commonly used for furniture because it is actually one of the hearty softwoods, performing almost as well as hardwoods like oak. Doug fir is peachy in color and has a linear but wide, smooth, and distinctive grain. All woods change in color over time, but Doug fir darkens drastically, and you can tell a piece is really well-worn if it's a burnt-umber color.

CHERRY
Domestic, Hardwood

Do we all know those shiny red cherrywood dining sets from the nineties? Yes. Did my parents buy one for my college apartment? Yes. Did I leave it on the sidewalk when I moved out? Yes. Do I want to talk about it? No. Poor cherry got such a bad rap because of some overzealous staining in the nineties and early aughts. Unstained, in its natural state, cherry is a beautiful light rust color with a fine, straight grain—a mid-toned, warm wood that should never be stained dark red again.

MAHOGANY
Exotic, Hardwood

Rich, gorgeous, Central and South American, deep brown, mahogany is the ultimate in luxury wood. Left outside to weather, it turns silver! However, because of illegal logging in tropical rainforests (where it grows), mahogany is terribly unsustainable and endangered. Steer clear unless you're buying something vintage.

TEAK
Exotic, Hardwood

Teak is grown in India and Southeast Asia and is used frequently outdoors because it can withstand weather well. A lot of vintage, mid-century, Danish woodwork (furniture and objects) are made in a rich, warm, dark teak that is now extinct. The color of the lumber correlates to the age of the tree, and older trees produce that famously beautiful dark mid-century teak. However, because of the popularity of the species in the fifties and sixties and because of unsustainable forestry practices, the old-growth trees are now extinct, leaving only young teak trees and lighter, yellowish lumber. Vintage teak is an amazing investment and a testament to the reasons we should be purposeful in our new wood purchases.

Profile: Brent Buck

1   Brent Buck's prized Dansk pepper mills displayed in a custom-built archway in his home. Brent was first drawn to these mills while thrifting with his wife; he prizes both the quality of the wood and their handmade aspect.

Coming from a long line of blue-collar tinkerers, Brent Buck grew up in rural Ohio making things with his hands, starting with wood toys as a kid and evolving to wood furniture in college. This is where he traces the origin of his staggering collection of vintage Dansk wood pepper mills—a collection several different people told me was not to be missed, and a collection that is displayed in a grand, custom-built archway in the architect's Brooklyn, New York, home.

"My first collection," Brent explains, "was of 'things that make things'—in other words, tools." Brent would scour flea markets and antiques shops for items that were clearly made by hand and for an express purpose: for example, an equestrian dental tool a farmer had made in the late 1800s out of cast brass. "The idea that a person had to solve a problem and make their own solution was deeply inspiring to me. It provided a feedback loop of making and utility that resonated with me as a designer."

The idea that a person had to solve a problem and make their own solution was deeply inspiring to me

In the process of searching for these oddities, he started to notice the recurring appearance of wood pepper mills. Manufactured by Dansk in the mid-century and fabricated by a somewhat obscure Danish woodworker, Richard Nissen, they were not an uncommon sight at the flea markets that Brent and his wife, Katie, were frequenting fifteen, twenty years ago. "You would always see one, and it would be, like, two dollars or something. So, we would buy it."

As a woodworker from a young age, intimately familiar with wood, Brent was blown away by the quality of the old-growth teak, and his curiosity was ignited. "We started keeping our eyes out for them, and we got so excited when we would find one. For me, collecting is less about 'owning the thing' than it is about 'finding the thing.' So once we got going, I started trading them and meeting other collectors and learning from them."

Growing his collection afforded Brent another unexpected joy. "I had moved to Brooklyn and no longer had a woodshop, but these pepper mills were small enough to work on [at home] and gave me the opportunity to go back to working with my hands. I've restored every pepper mill on the shelves. I've cleaned them, resanded them, and made them pristine, back to the condition as they would have been out of the box."

Brent believes that he owns every single design that was in production in the United States, and that his collection of Dansk pepper mills is complete. And because his greatest inspiration lies in the tools behind the tools and the makers of those tools, and because he's Brent Buck, he had to meet the maker. And so, he did. Brent and his wife flew to Denmark and knocked on Richard Nissen's door. Unsurprisingly, this was not something that anyone had done before. "I met Richard and went to Richard's house and saw Richard's woodshop. Richard's children came over [to me], and they said, 'No one's ever done this before! No one's ever asked to meet Richard!'"

During his visit, Richard brought Brent down to his basement studio, where the walls were lined with shelves of prototypes and designs, some of which had made it to production and others that had not.

A similar wall of models and materials exists in Brent's own architecture studio, the not-so-subtle parallel world to his collections, where Brent expends his energy as the maker behind the tools.

When asked about his architecture practice, Brent *casually* mentions that his studio's largest current project is a mass timber apartment building. Given the timing of a newly passed building code, forward-thinking clients, and a forward-thinking architect, Brent's project is set to be the first large-scale building in New York City that is built entirely of wood. "Everything is made out of wood," he explains. "The ceiling is wood, the floors are wood, the

2   Brent's collections extend beyond pepper mills: Here, three of his many Dinka headrests (solid wood carved pieces from South Sudan) have unique carvings that resemble lumbering animals lending their backs for your leisure.

1. WOOD

2

1. WOOD

2

3

4

5

6

1. WOOD

3   The studio along with all of the other dozen buildings on the Nakashima campus face south to maximize passive solar gain.

4–6 The Reception House was the last building on the campus that was designed by George and is a serene escape into mid-century Japan. The materials used were the finest available to him, and the luxury is at once evident and restrained.

My conversation with Mira Nakashima reveals a frank gratitude for the path that her father, the famed architect-turned-furniture-maker George Nakashima, put her on. One that followed his footsteps but also allowed for her to forge her own path both while he was alive and now that he's gone.

"When I was in fifth grade," Mira Nakashima reminisces, "one of the men in our shop took me under his arm, and he and his wife taught me to play my first instrument, the recorder. Several years and instruments later, I would sneak to the studio, where our piano lived, and I practiced. I practiced late at night all by myself. The sound resonates in the whole building, the instrument is grounded in the floor and becomes part of the architecture. It was a wonderful feeling, just riding the music to a place you've never been before.

"The poet Johann Wolfgang von Goethe said that architecture is frozen music, and that statement rings true to me. Both have an effect on human beings that is intangible. Nowadays people don't value that intangible essence of design as much. But I think Dad, in his quest to find his meaning and truth, eventually went into furniture because he realized furniture is small enough that you can have a true impact on human beings. You can create something that has a soul.

"When I was five, Dad asked me to help him build the stone wall in our first house. When I was in high school, I helped build the mock-up for the pool house. When I went to college, he insisted that I major in architecture, rather than linguistics or music, and then sent me to Japan to study architecture with some of his colleagues there. When I returned home from Japan, to my father's studio, the men in the shop became my best teachers and collaborators, as well as friends.

"This property, the workshop, and the studio represent and define the importance of hands-on building and architectural studies in furniture design. I've spent time making pieces in the workshop, oiling furniture in the finishing room, watching them come alive from plain pieces of wood to objects of beauty."

A LUMBER COLLECTION

"In the old days, my father used to purchase lumber rejects and improvise accordingly. Later, he was able to purchase logs scavenged by an arborist and have them custom-milled to his specifications. He also befriended a lumber supplier who provided him with large logs rejected from his veneer mills, allowed him to supervise their milling, then air-dry and then kiln-dry his lumber in Philadelphia until he had room to store it on the property here.

"After he died, there was so much lumber air-drying in Philadelphia that we had to build a new lumber shed here in New Hope. Selecting lumber from that large shed is sometimes quite an adventure. Two of our men spent the good part of a year 'rebuilding logs,' [that is,] finding the boards that came from one log, putting them back in the same sequence as they were once sawn, measuring, identifying species, photographing, and tagging them. We now have a much better idea of what is in the woodsheds. It is still a process trying to find the right piece of wood for each project, as each piece of wood from each tree has its own particular characteristics."

A STUDIO IN HARMONY

"When Dad spent time in India, he was immersed in the teachings of Sri Aurobindo. Dad believed in Integral Yoga, integrating the physical, mental, and spiritual in ourselves. Leaving architecture and going into furniture [making], he thought that he would be able to integrate the process of creating, doing away with typical work departments—engineering, design, sales, production—and reaching a harmony within the process of making furniture.

"Now that he's gone, we still adhere to that [idea of harmony], perhaps even more so. When he was here, the process was all a result of one man's drawing; now each project is the product of everyone in the studio and truly collaborative. I think this [collaborative spirit] reflects who *I* am and *my* nature."

---

7 George Nakashima

8 Mira Nakashima

9 Three buildings on campus are woodworking shops, one dedicated to finishing, and one solely devoted to chairs. Pictured here is the Main Shop.

10 To this day, there is not a formal delineation between George's and Mira's designs. Early George Nakashima chairs show the influence traditional Windsor chairs had on his sensibilities.

COLLECTED THOUGHTS

A piece of furniture made from wood represents the full life of the tree from which it came and all the hands of all the people who created it. When the circle of life is imparted on a natural element, it gains a soul.

Both Mira's and George's work has appreciated over time, making each piece far more valuable than it was when it was first created. Understanding a maker's motivations and philosophy can give you confidence that a purchase is both an acquisition and an investment.

7

8

9

10

53

2.

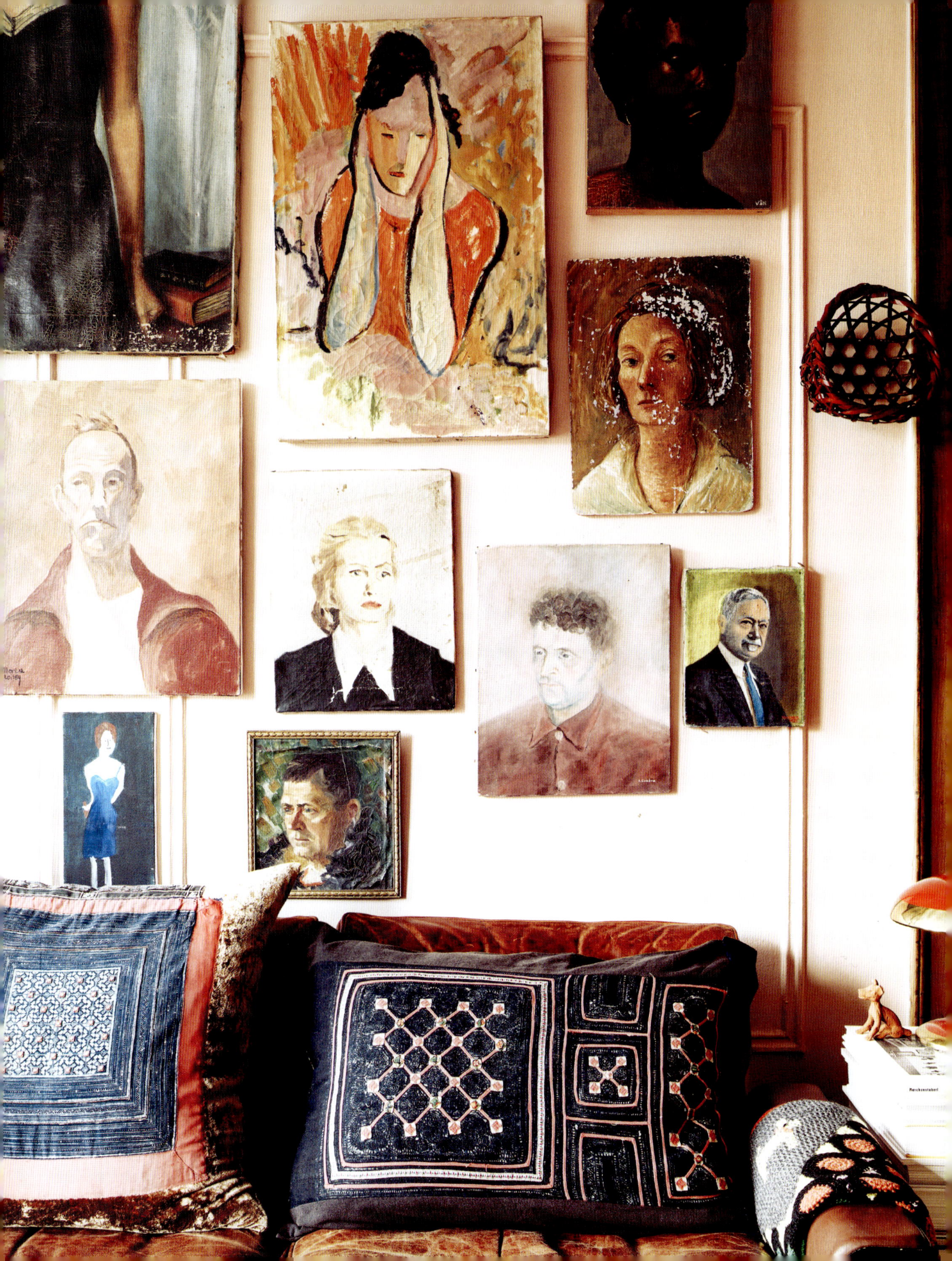

Fire

Fire is a starting point, an element that begets more elements. And many times, the result of a flame alight is more visible than the flame itself. Smoke signals, a stove sizzles, passion ignites into action toward our greatest accomplishments.

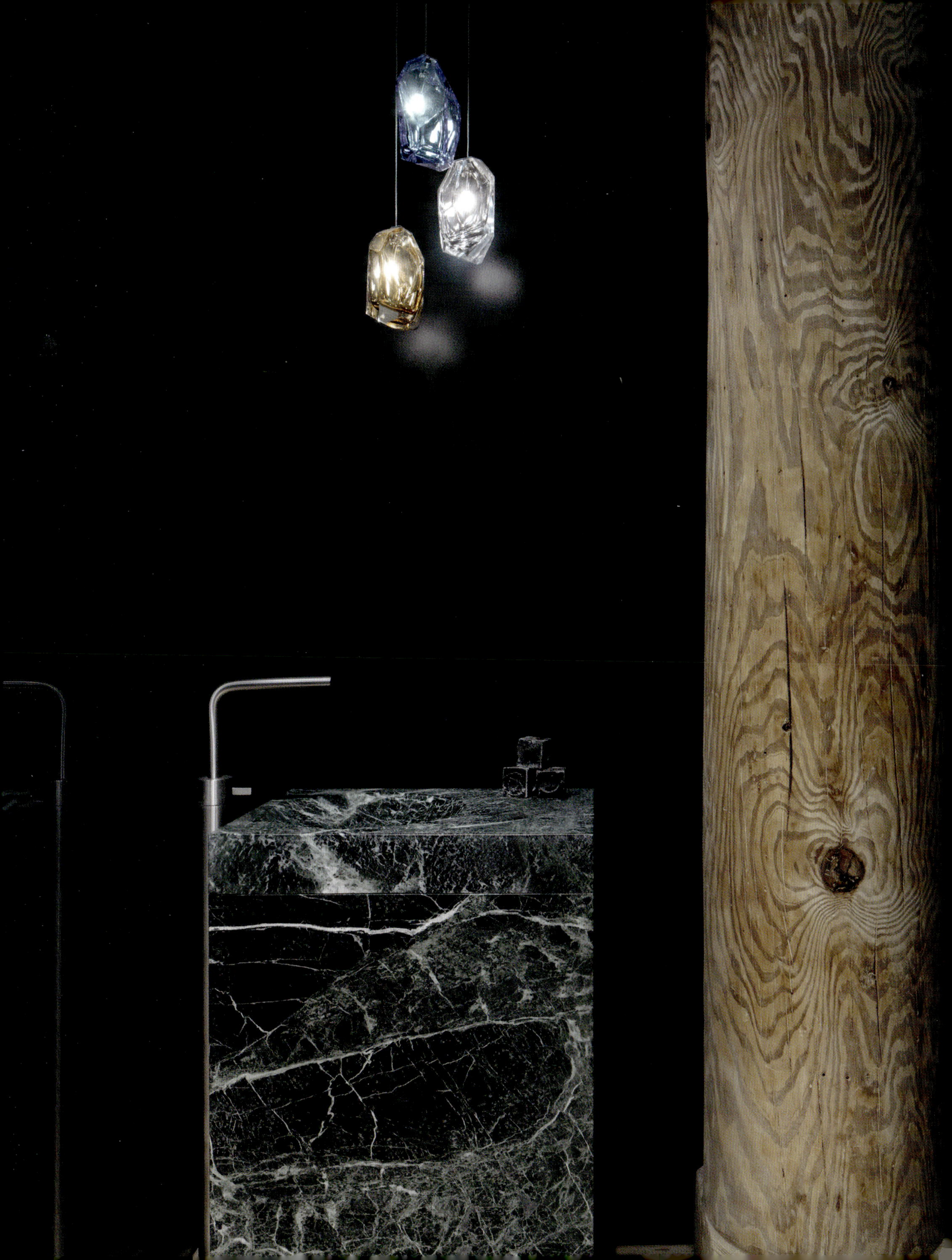

1

1 This heated holding chamber, lovingly called "the garage," is a kiln with doors that open and close. Glassblowers park their glass here while it's waiting to be used. Below sits a pipe warmer, where blow pipes heat up to the temperature needed to gather glass.

P. 54 Candelabras are sculptural, functional, collectible, and decorative. The centerpiece on this dining table in the foreground is actually a contemporary menorah.

P. 55 Found, traded, and thrifted portraits in the Speaklow living room evoke foggy, half-formed memories. The cushions on the sofa are handmade by Duy Pham.

P. 57 Handblown glass luminaries by Lasvit

(See page 206 for additional information.)

Is it any wonder that two of our most beloved materials, ceramic and glass, are born and completed through fire? It requires action to exist where other elements just "are."

One could argue that fire exists on a transcendent plane. That it provides us with a mystical element that beholds both the familiarity of warmth and the mystery of creation. Without fire, glass is sand, porcelain is dirt, love is a fable. Without fire, hope is a dream unrealized. The alchemy of fire is its innate imperative to transform.

IN THIS SECTION:

60 Speaklow: a collector, a minimalist, and the fire of love
64 How to Tame Fire
66 Deborah Czeresko blows hard and hot.
70 An architect and a chef make Lincoln Center cool again.
76 Stephanie H. Shih sculpts, then fires, porcelain food.
80 Michael K Chen's passion for contemporary art heats up his studio.

Profile: Speaklow

2. FIRE

1   Duy and Michael assemble a gallery wall that seems endless, yet somehow leaves us wanting more. Groupings range from random, to color coded to subject matter, and spacing is haphazard and spontaneous.

A lifelong collector and a decided minimalist fall in love, move in together, and start to sort through how their shared passion for the beautiful, the unique, and the delightful can cohabitate. While there are pages of stories that preface Duy Pham (the minimalist) and Michael Brown's (the collector) lives, this moment in time is where the absolute treasure that is their apartment started taking shape.

They treat the four-room home as their creative playground. Artworks, vintage finds, furniture, lighting, and books are puzzle pieces that sometimes interlock, sometimes repel, but are ultimately never staid. The walls behind their bed and sofa—on opposite ends of the apartment—each offer a master class on how to perfect a gallery wall. Not a measurement made, but every inch exudes emotion unspoken.

Curation and collecting take on a new meaning when every piece they acquire will live in their home but also eventually leave it.

"We love found objects, and we love found art. So much of our collection as it exists now is from our travels. We believe in the power of the stories behind the pieces. So much of art and design now is about who is on the label or how much something is worth. It takes the joy out of seeing things as they are. We try to be as innocent and curious as possible as we grow our collection.

"How can you be minimalist and maximalist all at once?" continues Duy, who concludes that their constant rotation of items, and the fact—arguably, the truly unique fact about their home—that they are open for appointments and (almost) everything is for sale, keep the space from oversaturation. Curation and collecting take on a new meaning when every piece they acquire will live in their home but also eventually leave it.

Michael and Duy call their space Speaklow. It's an open parlor for visitors to come and discover the men's viewpoint on what is worth keeping and for the duo to share the stories behind those objects. "We struggled for the longest time to define what we do. Are we collectors, are we curators, are we shopkeepers?" asks Duy. "But Michael texted me one day: 'We are collectors, curators, and caretakers of art, objects, and memories.'"

"Speak low when you speak, love," sings Billie Holiday in the namesake song that inspired Michael and Duy. "When you come to our home, we are sharing our passion and love with you. It's an intimate experience for our visitors and for us. The song implies and instructs us to speak at a volume that only the next person can hear."

2   Duy and Michael welcome people into their space with warmth and an infectious love of collecting.

3   A classic Akari lantern by Noguchi and a simple bouquet of spring flowers lighten the mood.

4   A nightstand should hold the most treasured of treasures.

5   A mantel full of treasures. Some are for sale and others (like the white rabbit), Michael says, "we're babysitting for a friend."

COLLECTED THOUGHTS

Michael and Duy connect many objects in their home to a person, a shared emotion, or a memorable experience, making their collection an evolving representation of their lives together.

Don't be afraid of a gallery wall. Exacting measurements should take a backseat to your gut intuition and emotional investment in each piece on display.

3

4

5

How to Tame Fire

- Candleholder but make it sculptural (aka a candelabra).
- Elegant and moody, tapered candles are like fresh-cut flowers: zero regrets, ever.
- Don't clean up your candle wax! Melted wax from tapered candles pool and drip, creating an unpredictable wax sculpture.
- Put a candelabra on a fireplace mantle and tame fire, on tamed fire.
- If you're lucky enough to have a fireplace mantle, use it. Put something, anything, on there. There is nothing sadder than a bare mantle.
- A mantle is the perfect picture shelf.
- The implication of fire is almost as heartwarming as actual fire. A slightly burnt wick, a black cast-iron fireplace cover, a pile of logs, all go a long way toward cozy.

1. Pairing a strong stone fireplace with delicate glass vessels and sconces results in an unexpected material juxtaposition.
2. A candelabra collection allows for constant reinvention of a dining table, a bookcase, a sideboard, and even a whole kitchen.

2

Studio: Deborah Czeresko

2. FIRE

1   Deborah Czeresko's studio is lined with glass experiments. An entire shelf of glass dog toys is intriguing because Deborah doesn't have a dog.

"[When] I walked into this [glassblowing] studio and saw a furnace, it was love at first sight. It seemed so mysterious. And then, when I tried to blow glass, I connected with the athleticism and artistry of it. I was really into the challenge and the sport of it; the aesthetics grew from there. That was the beginning."

Artist Deborah Czeresko found their stride in glassblowing in the eighties, even though men dominated the furnace at the time. "There was a lot of toxic masculinity in the studio back then. But I was very fortunate. A glassblower named William Gudenrath owned a private furnace, which was housed in a studio-glass nonprofit. William now works at the Corning Museum of Glass, but he's a goblet maker, the best of the best in New York. Back then he was looking for someone to clean his furnace after he was done. He let me use his furnace at night as long as I left him enough glass to do what he needed to do. I was very driven, so I practiced relentlessly, and that's how I learned."

Studio glass was such a rarified skill in the States, once you learned you were able to find work. "The highway was wide open at that point. It was only the beginning of the studio-glass movement in America. There weren't many people here who could create it, especially in New York. So as soon as I had any skill at all, the nonprofit where I was spending my nights practicing asked me to start teaching other people. So, at the beginning I earned money by teaching."

But how does a technician become an artist?

"The downtown scene in eighties' New York was like an open art book. Now-famous artists like Matthew Barney and Kiki Smith would come into the glass studio and make art. It was then that I started to see concepts applied to material.

"My first art project was an installation addressing the transformation of Ellis Island into a tourist attraction, glossing over its history of abusive medical examinations that immigrants were subject to upon arrival there. I felt it was really successful, and it was the first time I spoke to a social issue using my glassblowing abilities."

And from there, Deborah found themself toeing the line that many aspiring artists must toe: finding a way to stay the course of their creative convictions while also earning a living. In the early days they felt motivated and charged by the gay rights movement and work around the AIDS crisis. "It was happening to my community, and I felt compelled to do what I could."

Fast-forward years—no, decades—of glass making later, and Deborah answers an open casting call for the first season of a glassblowing-competition reality show called *Blown Away*. They are selected and, spoiler alert, they win. Deborah's final installation for the show is a subversive commentary on toxic masculinity and the role of women within it. Meat like a ham hock and a kielbasa hang beside a frying pan being *penetrated* by a link of sausages. Breaking the tension and the aggression of the meat are smooth, languid, sunny-side up eggs, including a giant, extra lounge-y egg right in the middle of it all.

Winning the show gained Deborah notoriety beyond what even the most successful glassblower could have expected in their career in the past—an incredible feat, considering that Deborah has stayed true to who they are throughout the process. Their work beyond the television show further explores their experience as a queer artist, with commentary on how the LGBTQIA+ community has thrived despite marginalization. "People have reached out to me to say that seeing someone like me in the studio, working with a furnace, gave them the courage to step toward one themselves. I've been able to see the change I had hoped for when I started in glass."

2   The hot shop furnance burns between 2,000 and 2,500 degrees and melts glass to a point of malleability.

3   Deborah and their assistant Ali Feeney have been working together for years, and you can tell by their dance.

4   After decades of experience, knowing when heated glass is ready for a specific treatment is a sixth sense for Deborah.

5   Deborah's tools need to be organized and at the ready. Once the glass is pulled out of the furnace, the work happens in a flash.

COLLECTED THOUGHTS

Handblown glass is a physical feat, and one that has been historically dominated by men. Seeking out work by nontraditional makers like Deborah can be a guidepost in collecting works imbued with meaning and subversion.

2. FIRE   68

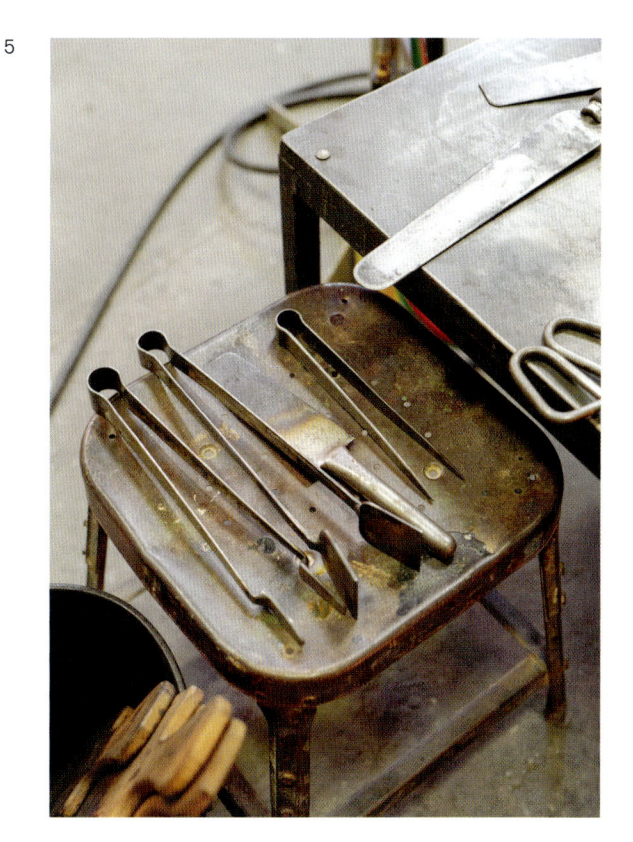

2

3

4

5

Profile: Preeti Sriratana

1

2. FIRE

1 Preeti Sriratana collects art from underrepresented artists, including the sculptural piece sitting over this credenza by Anthony Titus. "I'm embarrassed to say I don't know as much about art as I should. But I'm learning. There was something very visceral when I saw this piece for the first time."

Thai American architect Preeti Sriratana bookends his life through the lens of one event: the abrupt death of his maternal grandmother. "She was my best friend and my biggest supporter. I see my life in two chapters—one chapter when she was alive, and now I'm living the chapter without her. Her values, her priorities, they've become mine. Who she was then shapes who I am today."

"Ja," as Preeti and his siblings called her, was a much-needed cheerleader for the middling student growing up in the rural Midwest. "The first year we moved there, we weren't only the first Asians, we were the first people of color in the town." Different from the kids at school and disappointing his parents at home as a "solid B-minus student," Preeti found that Ja's love and support kept him somewhat unfazed by the racism that beset him as a young boy, and her death when he was sixteen left him reeling.

It was the memory of Ja's belief in him—and the sting that he was wasting it—that eventually motivated the largely unmotivated Preeti to apply himself and his natural inclination toward architecture. Bursting with untapped potential and a newly discovered work ethic, he found his way to grad school at Columbia and also found his first true home in the diverse and vibrant culture of New York City.

My collection is about feeling, a gut feeling when I see a piece.

Today, speaking to Preeti is speaking to the fully realized ideal of that potential, and an antidote to the isolation that can be so crushing for any young person who has felt utterly different from those around them. A founding partner at the pioneering design studio Modellus Novus, Preeti learned that his passion is not only for architecture but also for setting new precedents in how architecture is practiced. A diverse leadership team and staff—Preeti co-founded the firm with Jonathan Garnett, who is Black, and Steven Harper, who is white—are the stepping stones toward a grand ambition: "To design space for the many. The throughline of our work is that we strive to design spaces that welcome people from diverse backgrounds to gather and make [the spaces] their own."

At home, Preeti collects artwork by underrepresented Asian American and Black artists. "My collection includes these works from a series called *Walk with Me* by Kambui Olujimi." For six years, Mr. Olujimi turned his artistic practice into a meditation on one woman, a maternal figure, muse and mentor, whose portrait he re-created repeatedly 177 times in the wake of her untimely death. The portraits," Preeti says, "are so similar yet evoke and show so many different emotions." Preeti acquired twelve of them.

"My collection is about feeling, a gut feeling when I see a piece. When I saw this work, I related intensely to the agony of losing someone so close to you, but I also felt kindred to how to process and deal with the aftermath, what we take from the pain and the life of grief and growth afterward."

2　A painting by Chelsea Wong, which depicts a group of people coming together to celebrate the bounty of the ocean at sunrise, overlooks Preeti's view of Brooklyn.

3　Kambui Olujimi's piece *Walk with Me* is a mediation on an important maternal figure and mentor after her passing. The range of emotions drew Preeti into the piece, striking a chord with his own struggles with grief.

4　The view from the front door is this work by street photographer Martha Cooper. The photo (of a dance battle) represents all the different people of New York coming together to make the city their own.

5　Tatiana restaurant, designed by Preeti's studio, Modellus Novus, celebrates transparency and visibility of service with an open kitchen that can be seen from all of Lincoln Center.

COLLECTED THOUGHTS

Collecting from the gut leads us to places otherwise unexplored and gives us a physical and sensory connection to the trials and triumphs that make us whole.

2. FIRE

2

3

4

5

73

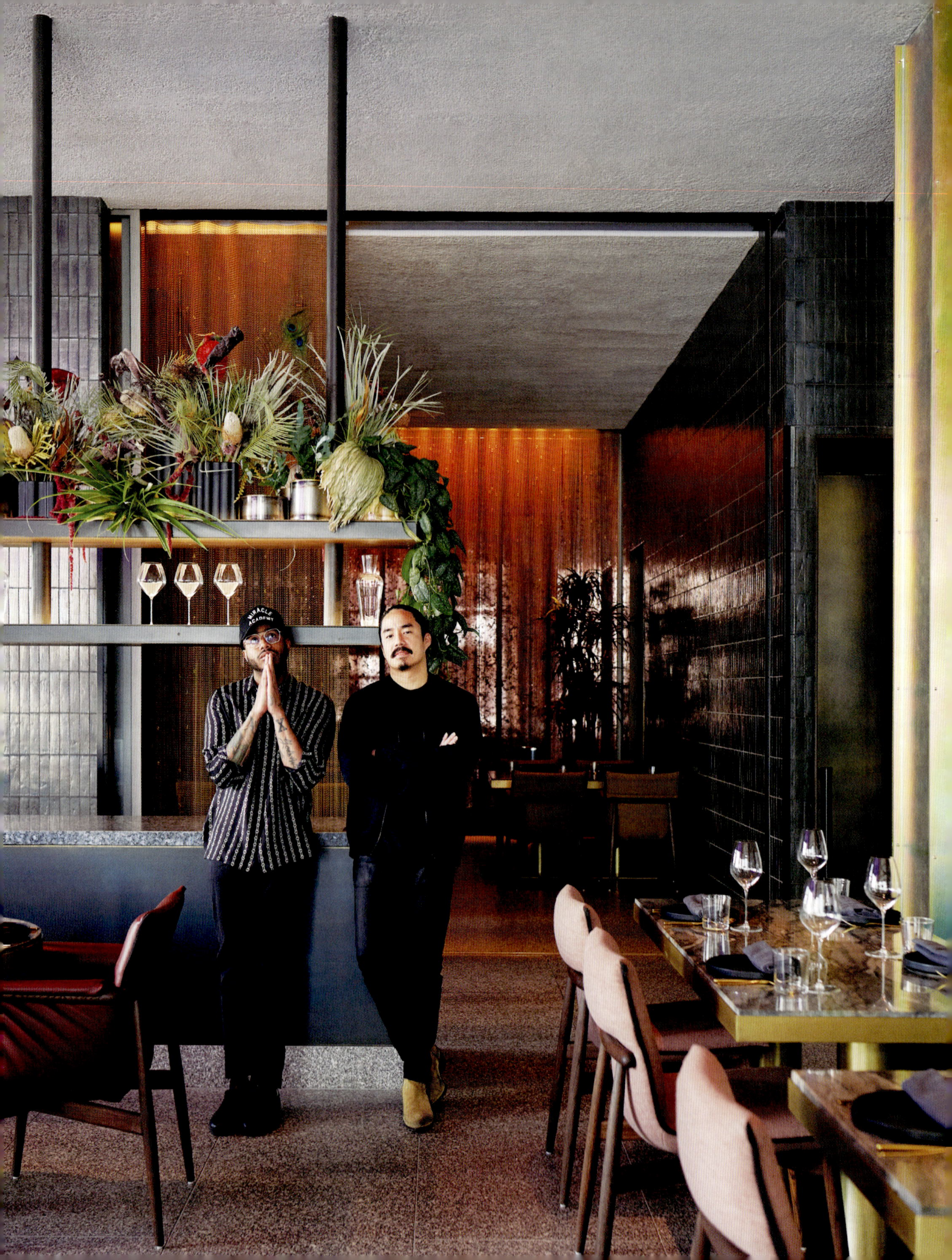
MIRACLE
ACADEMY

Fire in the Fringes

1   Kwame and Preeti are kindred spirits in that they both see themselves as outsiders in parallel industries that thrive on a certain status quo.

"It's named after my sister," says chef Kwame Onwuache of Tatiana, his restaurant in New York City's Lincoln Center designed by Preeti and his studio. "The menu is inspired by the food I grew up eating with her."

As kids, Kwame and Tatiana would traverse the culinary city on a budget: lunch-special sushi, food-cart shawarma, hermetically sealed brownies from the corner bodega. All this food he stowed in his memory banks for years until the opening of her namesake restaurant, when he pulled them out and used them as the starting point for a menu that has earned Kwame both critical acclaim and a packed house night after night.

Like Preeti, Kwame identifies as an outsider in an industry that isn't always kind to its fringes, and when it came to Tatiana he insisted on full creative control. "He was given final say by the board of directors at Lincoln Center on everything, which is not a small feat for any chef," says Preeti. And so the restaurant is full of details that are appreciated by designers and diners alike, inventive finishes and furnishings that elevate the space and promptly step aside, making room for the experience of being there, the experience of the meal. With nary a detail left unturned, the crux of the design is based on transparency. Every corner of the restaurant is visible from the grand, central courtyard of Lincoln Center. Even the kitchen is open on not one but two sides, allowing patrons of the ballet or opera the opportunity to peek into the inner workings of Kwame's kitchen, and subsequently his mind.

COLLECTED THOUGHTS

"There is a line from Kwame's memoir," says architect Preeti Sriratana, "from which we drew inspiration while designing this restaurant: 'Invisible men and invisible women making invisible food for invisible children.' Our goal was to bring them forward and not only reveal them, but [also] celebrate and exalt them at Tatiana." Pieces in a collection can do the same for the artists who created them.

Tatiana is a harmonic collaboration between Preeti and Kwame, two outsiders collecting food memories, sentiments, and emotions over the span of their careers, taking something internal, intangible, even soulful, and creating something experiential, tactile, and wholly new.

Studio: Stephanie H. Shih

2. FIRE

1   Stephanie Shih's ceramics studio has remnants of her soy sauce collection, bottles that acted as models for the pots she made in their likeness. "I count the Veri Veri Teriyaki as soy sauce. It counts."

"I made the dumplings, I posted the dumplings, the dumplings got some attention, and non-Asian people were telling me that I should start answering my phone 'May I take your order?'" ceramicist Stephanie H. Shih says of the beginning of her art practice. After over a decade of working as a creative director and copywriter in corporate America, Stephanie made some porcelain dumplings—that look *exactly* like real dumplings—and their organic success gave her the opportunity to step into the life of a full-time artist.

They also put Stephanie right in the little-traversed intersection of art, cuisine, and racial-identity politics. The popularity of the dumplings created an uneasy momentum—people telling her to make them look like they'd been dipped in soy sauce, the "May I take your order" fiasco, suggestions to sell them in wax paper sleeves associated with Chinese takeout. Stephanie's response, and the evolution of her work, is a testament to the breadth of her reach as an artist and to her rejection of any quick answers or shortcuts to racial identity in America today.

"It's too simple to only talk about race when it comes to the dumplings. Really, I was trying to move away from the idea that they were novelty objects and instead tie them to the cuisine and culture. So the first 'condiment' I made was black vinegar, because it's not widely known in the States that black vinegar is much more important to the dipping sauce than soy sauce. Then I made a chili crisp and a sesame oil."

Stephanie collected over thirty bottles of different types of real soy sauce as reference for her work.

You see, the elephant in the room is the soy sauce. Stephanie collected over thirty bottles of different types of real soy sauce as reference for her work, and there are still a handful of lifelike ceramic soy sauce pieces lining her studio shelves that haven't sold to collectors. "I held off on making it [the soy sauce] for a long time, and when I did, I made a gallon jug that would be less familiar to people who weren't from Asian households. Then I made a whole show that was only soy sauce. I made thirty different kinds from all over Asia. If I was going to make soy sauce, I was going big."

Stephanie has a complicated relationship with her early work—the dumplings and condiments project is from 2018—and today she worries that its popularity may inadvertently contribute to grouping the Asian diaspora into a flat entity pitted against white supremacy. To Stephanie, the reality is far more nuanced: "I'm trying to push back on the idea that authenticity and culture are fixed. You can't put a hard border around what's authentic or not, because there is no culture that remains untouched by other cultures."

To follow her career, as I have, is to watch the growth and self-reflection of a progressive thinker finding new ways to communicate her internal dialogue about what it means to be a minority woman in the American art world. Stephanie's work stays largely within the realm of Asian groceries, but it challenges what that actually is. Seemingly disparate Western food items like Spam and Royal Dansk butter cookies are so ubiquitous to Asian American households, they require no explanation for many of us but must seem confusingly random to others.

The work is as visually delightful as it is thought-provoking, proving *my* thesis that the most powerful work in the art and design realm is that which is both meaningful and beautiful. Stephanie's just-left-of-lifelike objects draw you in and then give you pause on why you love them. "Rather than shame people for not agreeing with me, I'm making work that exemplifies how I think about culture as a way to, hopefully, get them to think a little more broadly.

"My collection and the soy sauce project are really about cultural interchange. It was early in my thinking about how we define borders, and how cultural borders are a construct of our perception."

2   Four of Stephanie's soy sauce pots at a solo exhibit at Berggruen Gallery in San Francisco

3   Stephanie notes, "The first condiment I made was black vinegar, because it's not widely known in the States that black vinegar is much more important to dipping sauce than soy sauce."

4   Stephanie Shih

5   Steph's studio is a display of personal inspiration that ranges from political to cultural. Childhood memories, family friends, and comic-strip clippings share space with color swatches and ceramic-specific technical notes.

COLLECTED THOUGHTS

Stephanie's soy sauce collection was born out of a desire to share the nuances of culture and cuisine. "I'm trying to push back on the idea that authenticity and culture are fixed," she says. "You can't put a hard border around what's authentic or not, because there is no culture that remains untouched by other cultures."

Embrace the subject. If something speaks to you and your passions, don't be afraid to go big! Stephanie's soy sauce collection topped 30-plus bottles and was the starting point for a body of work that was an important inflection point within her career.

2

3

4

5

Studio: MKCA

2. FIRE

1   MKCA is home to Michael K Chen's collection of design and art, including *Bungalow* (2022) by Chiffon Thomas, hanging from a nearly invisibile cable. Chiffon is a trans man who grew up in an ultra-conservative family, and these sculptures are gothic houses made from the leather covers of Bibles. Also pictured, a credenza by Christopher Kurtz and photographs from John Baldessari's series *Throwing Three Balls in the Air to Get a Straight Line (Best of Thirty-Six Attempts)*.

COLLECTED THOUGHTS

Michael doesn't overthink his collection; rather, he is unapologetic about what interests him philosophically and aesthetically. This has led to a genuine group of works that reflect what he finds most compelling in life, design, and art.

"My first introduction to what contemporary art could do and mean was as an undergrad when I interned as a curatorial assistant for an incredible curator named Lawrence Rinder," says Michael K Chen, the beautifully inspired architect and interior designer behind MKCA. "It coincided with learning more about work that other queer artists were making in the late eighties and early nineties during the height of the AIDS epidemic. It was artists like Félix González-Torres and David Wojnarowicz who were able to articulate fear and love and rage in beautiful and poignant and powerful ways. I was a young, somewhat recently out gay kid, just trying to understand my place in the world, and these artists grabbed me in such an affecting way, and I don't think I've ever let that experience go.

"With my own collection, it's not a conscious or deliberate thing. I'm interested in artists, not just their works. I'm interested in artists' and designers' trajectories, their histories, their backgrounds, and because of that, I find diversity and identity to be really interesting. I find that to be interesting in general. I love conceptual work, but I also find art making to be so courageous unto itself that an artist putting their self on the line on top of everything else is deeply moving to me."

2. FIRE

2   A shelf holds a collection of vessels by designer Cody Hoyt.

3   In the studio, tonal walls create a sense of divided space without doors or true rooms. *Shine Light into Dark Places*, by Thai artist Rirkrit Tiravanija, plays with typography and social practice. The artist is known for his work with food preparation and communal meals, and the print hangs in the studio's kitchenette.

4   Michael Chen sits on a vintage red sofa by Takahama Kazuhide for Knoll. *Fauna V*, by Gabriel Rico, hangs on the wall behind him.

5   MKCA's work reflects Michael's passion for art with fearless use of color and reverent placement of vintage pieces.

3.

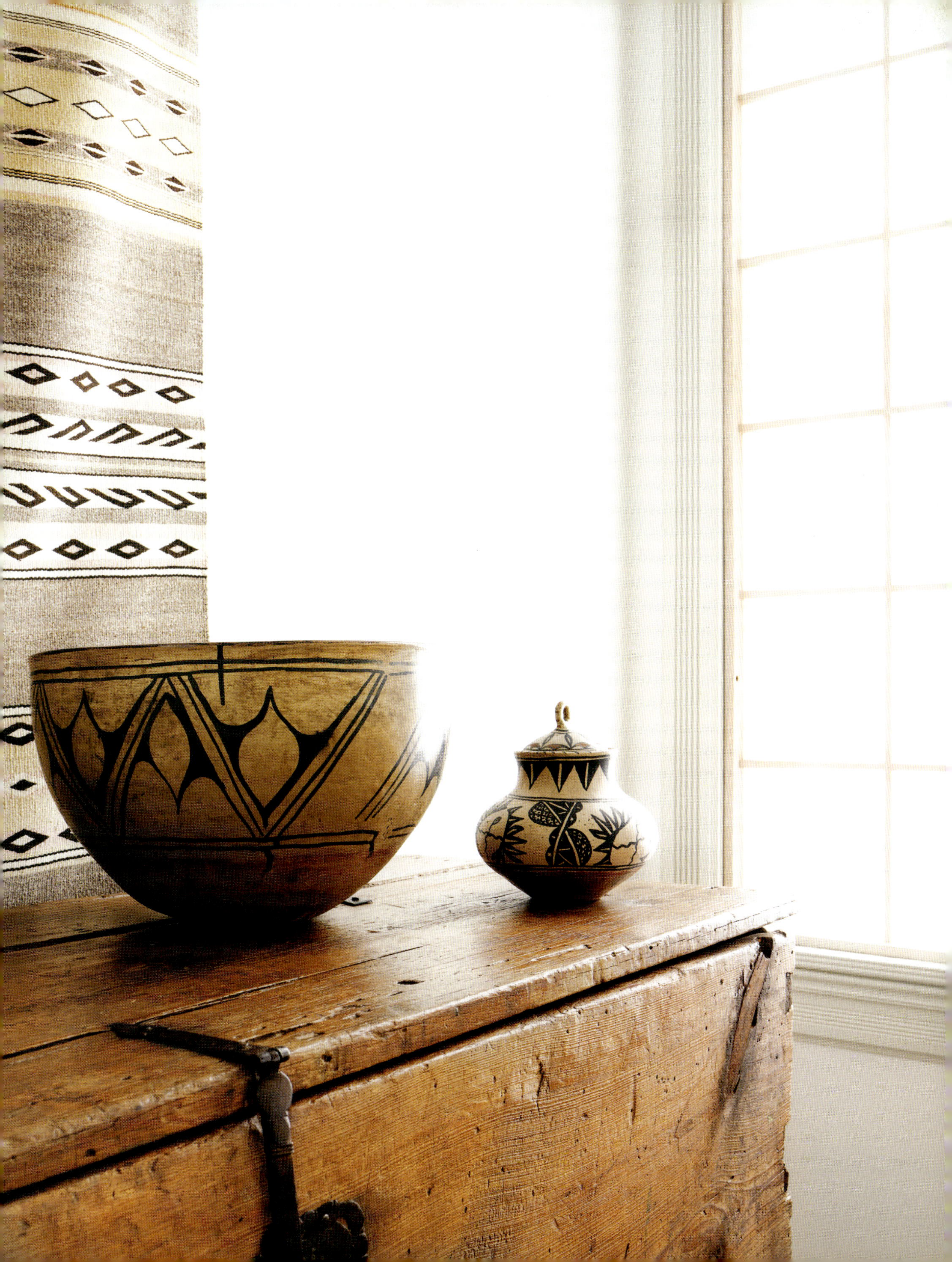

Earth

Let's be honest, parsing materials and processes into separate elements belies the unsaid truth that everything comes from the earth. Without her, we would be particles, floating aimlessly in the abyss.

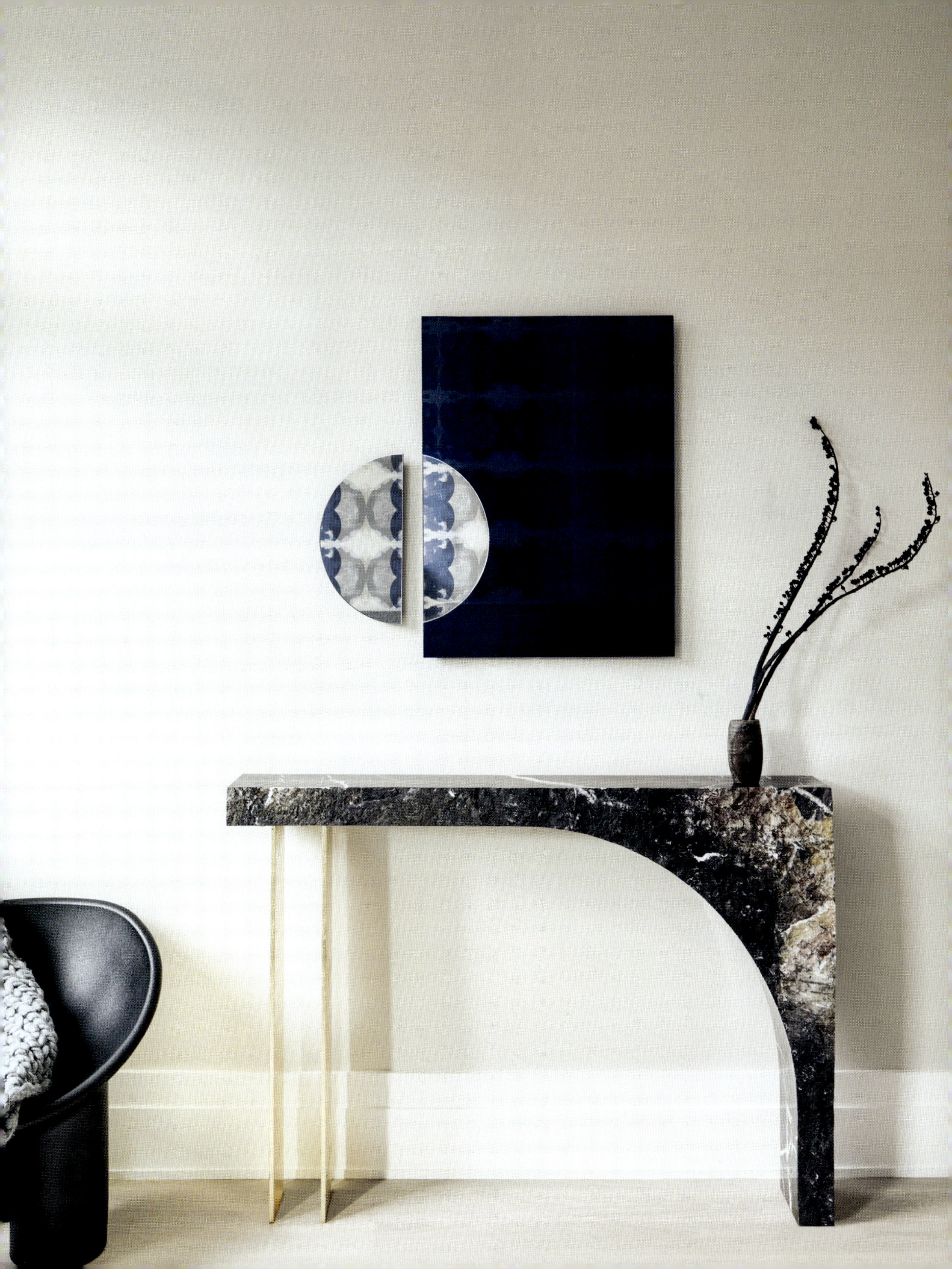

1

1   This collection of stools includes many varieties, and stacking them low, in front of the window, avoids the pitfall of clutter. Another key to the success of the display is variety: If every piece is interesting, the viewer feels less overwhelmed by the whole.

P. 84   This ottoman by Kelly Wearstler has "real" feet.

P. 85   Antique pieces from Shiprock Santa Fe

P. 86   Textile sculpture by Elodie Blanchard, from the collection of Dania Ahmad

P. 87   A mirror by Nina Cho and stone console by A Space

(See page 206 for additional information.)

But alas, not every word of every chapter of every book can be dedicated to the mother to whom we owe our existence. So we start here with those that are closest to her, carefully altered, and most true:

> Fiber, plucked from the earth, spun into yarn, and woven into art.
> Plants themselves, bringing the untamed world inside.
> Earthen ceramics, gathered from around the world.

The honesty of this work is not to intimate a lack of precision, in fact the opposite. The human hand, when applied with care and deference to material can take something magnificent and make it limitless.

IN THIS SECTION:

90   Antique Japanese folk textiles
96   Buy textiles online with confidence.
98   Textile artist Hiroko Takeda and her beautiful looms
104 How to collect brushes
106 Quilter Meg Callahan wrestles with bringing more "stuff" into the world.
112 Baring it all while staying grounded.
114 Down-to-earth tastemakers Benjamin Reynaert and Carly Cushnie share their collections.
118 Leyden Lewis's collections speak to the heart (and the essence) of things.
122 A rare cacti collection sparks inspiration.
126 Humor and style rule this designer's animal kingdom.
132 The "body" of a collection
134 Maya Schindler's collections are memories and earthen heirlooms.

Profile: Sri Threads

[1]

3. EARTH

1   Gauzy Japanese textiles define Stephen Szczepanek's home, which doubles as a showroom for his collection, Sri Threads. Stephen's collection includes Japanese and Indian relics, which he displays with reverence to each culture.

"For me, the word 'expert' is an expanding function. We're all learning. The more I learn, the more I realize how much I didn't know."

Stephen Szczepanek, by all measures, is an expert. He has been collecting antique Japanese folk textiles for over twenty years and, under the name Sri Threads, sells them out of his home gallery. When he was first introduced to the boro textiles that have become his specialty—*boro* comes from a Japanese word that means tattered and repaired—he recognized them for the innate beauty in their utility. "There was a strong resemblance to modernist or contemporary art in these textiles. Folk art collectors were not collecting Japanese folk art [at the time], but they recognized boro textiles as these anonymous pieces that were artful while lacking the intention to create art.

"I felt an immediate kinship with it. I completely understood it molecularly. I saw it, and I got it. It was very easy for me to get into this field, because I automatically felt like I was embracing it and it was embracing me. I started with what I could [afford], buying online and from dealers. When I was finally able to catapult myself to go to Japan, that was when I really started my education. I was able to talk to people closer to the primary source, and [I] started to understand the different hallmarks and keynotes that exist within each typology. Categories that are collectible, beautiful, and essential for a good collection."

"[I] started to understand the different… categories that are collectible, beautiful, and essential for a good collection."

Where Sri ends and Stephen begins is a blurry line. To step into his gallery is to step into his home, and it is also to be transported to another place and time from where you entered. Not only are there stacks upon stacks of his textile collection for sale, but there are also remnants of a past in craft that looks, feels, and smells like old Japan (or a conjured memory of it): rice paper stencils, hand-carved

2

3

2–4 Boro comes from a Japanese word that means tattered and repaired. When Stephen discovered these textiles, he recognized the innate beauty in their utility and felt immediate kinship with the work. Now, he fervently collects boro textiles along with (visually arresting) related tools and historic documents.

4

print blocks, and notebooks with scraps of indigo-dyed fabrics affixed neatly to each page.

"I think the best kind of collector embraces the subject and knows it well. Then is able to be capricious in collecting," Stephen says. "You want to collect the great and interesting pieces, but you also want to collect things that talk to you personally. One of the beauties of collecting is that you can play a little.

5   Garments are displayed with a dowel, showcasing the textile and workmanship in its full glory.

> "I think the best kind of collector embraces the subject and knows it well. Then is able to be capricious in collecting."

"I've been able to expand my education around the pillars of what I believe make antique folk textiles interesting. I've been able to identify a lineage of processes and uses that influenced one another through time, and I work to build a comprehensive collection that paints a panorama of the history of these textiles. I'm still working on it."

COLLECTED THOUGHTS

Educating yourself is the unsung hero of collecting. Once you start to understand where something comes from and what its purpose was (and is), you will start to instinctively understand its value.

3. EARTH

5

How to Understand Textiles Online

Whether you're purchasing clothing, a pillow, a rug, or even yards of fabric online, it can be nerve-wracking to know exactly what you're getting without seeing and feeling it in person. Not to worry: There are a few informational cues and keywords that let you know what you'll be getting, whether it's a brand-new piece or a well-loved vintage item.

Material content: There are two big categories, and a lot of gray area, when it comes to fabric content. Generally, fibers—the fluff that is spun into thread—are either synthetic or natural. Synthetics, such as polyester, nylon, and elastane, are much more durable than natural fibers but have a colder, crispier surface feel and can often look a little shiny. Because of the lack of water retention in synthetics, they have a lot of static. Natural fibers like cotton, linen, wool, and silk have a softer hand feel but are also much easier to damage through wear and tear. There are blended fabrics that use both natural and synthetic fibers to give us the best of both worlds: soft fabric that is also durable. If you see a blended fabric, you can bet that the larger the percentage of particular fibers, the more that piece takes on the characteristic of either a natural or synthetic cloth.

Weighted words: While there isn't a standard rating system for the weight of fabric for normal consumers like us, there are words that clue us in on how heavy a fabric is.

1   The Shiprock Santa Fe gallery is rooted in the art, tradition, and culture of the Navajo and other Indigenous tribes of the Southwest. Owners Jed and Samantha Foutz's collections include Navajo rugs and blankets, Native American jewelry, Pueblo pottery, as well as sculpture, basketry, and art by leading Native American artists.

2   Boro textiles are ofen smiliar in weight to poplin and natural fiber fabrics like cotton and linen.

1

3. EARTH

VOILE
Voile is one of the lightest weights out there. Voile is sheer, meaning you can see through it.

POPLIN
Poplin is medium/lightweight and crisp. Men's dress shirts are often made of poplin.

TWILL
Twill is a weave that can range from medium to heavy weight, but the word usually refers to a medium weight fabric with a subtle diagonal textured rib.

CANVAS
Canvas is a heavy fabric like thick denim.

PRINTED VS. JACQUARD
A pattern in a textile is either printed on top of or incorporated into the weave, the latter called jacquard. You can tell a jacquard pattern because the back of the textile will show some version, usually the inverted colors, of the pattern. Printed patterns don't show on the back side of the textile. Because of the construction needed to weave a jacquard, they are medium weight to heavy, while printed textiles range from light to heavy.

Studio: Hiroko Takeda

[1]

3. EARTH

[1] As a child, Hiroko Takeda thought her toy loom was the key to unlock the world, and through the course of her career, she has discovered she wasn't far off.

"I was eight or nine years old and walking through a toy store. I saw a toy loom and thought, *Wow, that loom can make fabric?! Amazing!* So I asked for it as my birthday or Christmas present. I remember thinking, *If I get this, my life will be set*. It turns out that weaver and textile artist Hiroko Takeda's nine-year-old self was on to something.

Hiroko grew up to study textiles at Joshibi University of Art and Design in a department steeped in the tradition of the Mingei, or folk-art, movement—the philosophy that art and beauty can exist in everyday, utilitarian objects. Because of the program at Joshibi, Hiroko's early education was grounded in technicality and rusticity. "I spun yarn, washed wool, and made fleece. I learned to hand-dye yarn. I learned intensely technical skills around the traditional craft of textiles."

And her work today hints at this start she had in her very hands-on, skill-based early education and professional life. While her pieces are inspiringly artful, Hiroko's weavings have a complexity about them that only a master technician could dream of achieving.

"I saw a toy loom and thought, *Wow, that loom can make fabric?!*"

"I worked as a technical designer for a commercial interior textile company in Kyoto. It was good for me at the time, almost like a game of how to make textiles most efficiently. Eventually, though, I started to realize that I was limited in my abilities. That there was a world of beautiful textiles and techniques that I wasn't familiar with. So I decided to go to graduate school."

Hiroko packed up and moved to London, attending the Royal College of Art and thus starting down a path of discovery and growth in her medium of weaving. She soon won a competition and a seat in the legendary textile designer Jack Lenor Larsen's studio, which eventually landed her in New York City.

"He wasn't my mentor," she says frankly. "But we were able to talk at length about weaving and weaving structure in a way others in the studio couldn't, because he was just so revered. I cherish the time I was able to spend with him, when he asked me about Japan, my experience at Joshibi—he was closely associated with the leaders of the Mingei movement who were the founders of my department at school. He took an interest in the younger generation of weavers."

By the time Hiroko set out on her own, her aesthetic sensibility was already established. She knew what her definition of beauty was, and she knew how to create it with her loom. Her pieces are soaring and grounded, technical and fantastical, and she has garnered collectors and followers from across the fields of design, architecture, and fashion.

"Weaving is so technical. I am constantly trying new things and learning more about my medium. This trial and error, learning and growth, it feeds the creativity and the art. I'm always learning and as a result I grow as an artist."

Just as her skill and art are cumulative, so are her looms. In her studio now sit four magnificent looms, works of art themselves. One of them she inherited from her non-mentor Jack Larsen. "The studio gave me a loom when they [left New York and] moved to Paris. I still use it a lot. Very stable settings, and a nice loom. A very nice loom."

2 Threads and tools line Hiroko's studio shelves.

3 Hiroko Takeda's studio has four large looms, one of which was gifted to her by Jack Larsen Studio.

4–5 Textile art has transcended its craft moniker and come into its own as a highly collectible art form. Hiroko's work is sought-after for its tactility, intricacy and nuance; it is art that adds texture to a room.

COLLECTED THOUGHTS

Collections can also be the tools of your trade. For a textile artist, a treasured loom turns into a business, and evolves into a studio where Hiroko's growing collection of looms are creating textiles for new collectors of her works.

The process often becomes a valuable and irreplaceable asset for an artist. "I am constantly trying new things and learning more about my medium. This trial and error, learning and growth, it feeds the creativity and the art."

3. EARTH

2

3

4

5

101

6

7

6–7   Tools of the trade are artful in and of themselves. Shuttlecocks, crafted from solid wood, and a skein-winder are essential to the weaving process.
8   A cork board serves as a dimensional diary of samples and weaving experiments.

8

How to Collect Brushes

- Don't expect that they will sweep dirt.
- Don't expect that they will sweep anything.
- Mostly they should sit there and look rustic and pretty.
- Sometimes they can lie on their side.
- A handmade brush wins every time.
- But really, any brush will do.

1   Brushes in a line create a beautifully varied, yet satisfyingly uniform, display on a bathroom shelf.

2   Using the triangular fan of a brush and the skinny cylinder of the handle, you can create a geometric display—whether hanging from a hook or lying atop a coffee table.

3–4   Interesting begets interesting: When you have clever and rare pieces in your collection, put them on display where everyone can see.

1

3. EARTH

2

3

4

Studio: M. Callahan

1

3. EARTH

1   A Victorian New England house, replete with original details and charm, is where Meg Callahan spends her professional time as a quilter. Meg is a contemporary designer with reverence for the rich history of quilts; her studio is a perfect microcosm of her creative universe.

"The first quilt I ever made was in home economics," says Meg Callahan, a contemporary designer whose medium of choice is sprawling, geometric, jaw-dropping quilts. "It was a 'Quillow': a quilt that folded up and tucked into a pillow," Meg explains while folding an imaginary blanket, hand over hand, ending with a smooth, forward, five-finger slide, indicating the final tuck.

I've known Meg for years—she was one of the first designers who said yes to joining Colony. But after all this time, I never knew that her first piece was the sewing equivalent of a spork.

What I did know was that Meg grew up in Oklahoma, that she graduated from RISD, and that the day after I drove from New York City to a coffee shop in Providence, Rhode Island, and convinced her to join Colony, she embarked on a one-way cross-country road trip with no idea where she would end up.

...

The road trip eventually landed Meg in Seattle, where she moved in with her sister. She split her time between making quilts and working for a local apparel company as a production manager, occupying two diametrically opposite worlds. "Manufacturing is about speed, efficiency, and output, while my quilts are purposely slow and deliberate. Quilting is very challenging, but there's a lot of pride in that. Almost a clout," says Meg about her passion for the endeavor. "I became interested in quilting when I was at RISD and was examining pattern as structure—things like chain-link fencing. I made my first quilt (second only to Quillow) as part of a larger project, and it spoke to me. It felt like a discovery of an object that has so many dimensions. A quilt can be activist, gender-centric or genderless, very democratic, very crafty. It can be community made or individually made. From Quillow to my first real quilt to now, it never stopped being interesting. I'm always so excited to do the next one."

But the work she did in production wasn't lost on her, either.

"I find manufacturing to be really fascinating because there has to be a lot of creative problem-solving in making something at volume while keeping it cost-effective. But I do think that a lot of that creativity gets lost because of the overpowering need for more efficiency," she admits.

...

Fast forward: I was talking to Meg. She didn't sound like the optimistic and measured Meg I knew; she sounded frantic. She was sorry, she said. She didn't think she wanted to make quilts anymore, she said. "I don't feel right just putting more *stuff* into the world, when everything feels in peril."

...

When you work closely with someone, and you also know their work so intimately, you tend to feel surprised when truths are later uncovered about the time you spent working together. This is how I felt when Meg described the start of her design studio as a rolling snowball she had no control over. That first quilt was staggering and beautiful and garnered attention that led to New York City shows, to orders for more quilts, to Colony, to Seattle, and ultimately to a game of quilt catch-up. She told me later that she didn't feel like she had made those choices, but more that she was reacting to opportunities she felt she couldn't turn down. It's no wonder, then, that a few years later, she was overcome by a crisis of faith. She really wasn't sure why she was making quilts as a business anymore.

A quilt can be activist, gender-centric or genderless, very democratic, very crafty. It can be community made or individually made.

"It's like history braiding together," she says while acknowledging her desire to stop back then and describing where she is today. "The snowball has stopped rolling, but I'm rebuilding my studio with mindfulness. I am inspired by the structure and output of large-scale manufacturing, as well as the community-based manufacturing in Seattle. I'm working to combine that structure with quilting as a centerpiece."

2 Meticulously planned samples and drawings are an essential part of the quilting process.

3 The studio is in a Victorian house, shared with other designers and creatives, in downtown Providence, Rhode Island.

4 The sewing machine, the VIP of the studio.

2

3

4

5

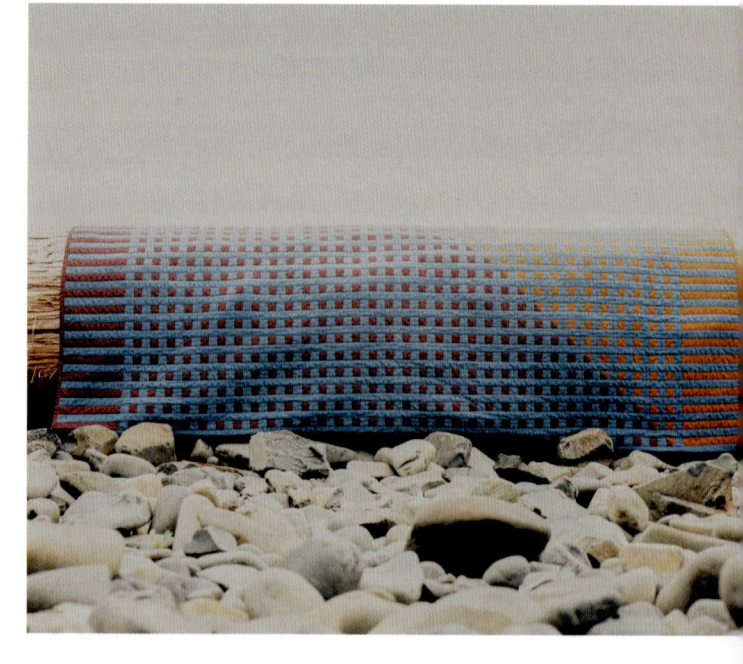

6 7

3. EARTH

5   An early quilt by Meg captures her wandering spirit and intensely considered respect for our environment.

6   A photo by Rinne Allen from Meg's photography project: She gifted three quilts to three photographers to live with for a year, and to photograph.

7   Photographer Robin Stein's shots of Meg's quilts incorporate nature in a juxtaposition between geometric patterns and organic settings.

8   Photographer Rachael Larkin's quilt made its way around Los Angeles.

And she still hasn't abandoned the quilt as an endlessly interesting object. In her first project back after her self-imposed hiatus, Meg lent three previously made quilts to three photographers to live with for a year. The barter was that they photograph the quilts in use over the course of that year. The results are a stunning series of warmly lit, real-life moments that are inhabited, accentuated, and defined by the presence of Meg's quilts. We exhibited two of the quilts alongside their photographs at Colony, wrinkled, slightly faded, with a few stains here and there. We purposely didn't wash or press them for display. The used quilts, in my opinion, were two of the most beautiful works that we had shown of Meg's to date.

And therein lies the answer to Meg's question. Why put more stuff into the world when everything is in peril? Because her craft, her art, her business, her production, occupies a rare and honest space: an overlap of art, utility, and humanity. And the very act of living with her work defines its value.

COLLECTED THOUGHTS

Contemporary quilters like Meg are bringing the traditional American craft into a new realm. Collectible quilts of the past have represented domesticity, but Meg is using her art to make a statement about societal norms, consumption, and mass production. This is not your grandmother's quilt collection.

8

How to Bare It All

- Clutter is the enemy; the junk drawer (or closet!) is your friend.
- Favorite art books stack to make the perfect little pedestal for an objet d'art.
- Keep it fresh by rotating pieces from your collection in and out of sight.
- Make friends with a bar cart.
- Pinboard, but make it chic.
- When in doubt, find a theme. Color is a good place to start, but the sky's the limit (gifts from your mom, things you saved from elementary school, Europe).
- It's pronounced "chotch-key."

1   Benjamin Reynaert's tonal pinboard displays inspiration, mementos, and correspondence.

2   A collection of tea kettles is proudly on display on this open kitchen shelving. A mixture of patterns, materials, and shapes makes for a textured display.

3   Family history, personal triumphs, and joyful travels are all represented on this open bookcase. Lower shelves are home to books and less delicate items—the kinds that can't break.

3. EARTH

3

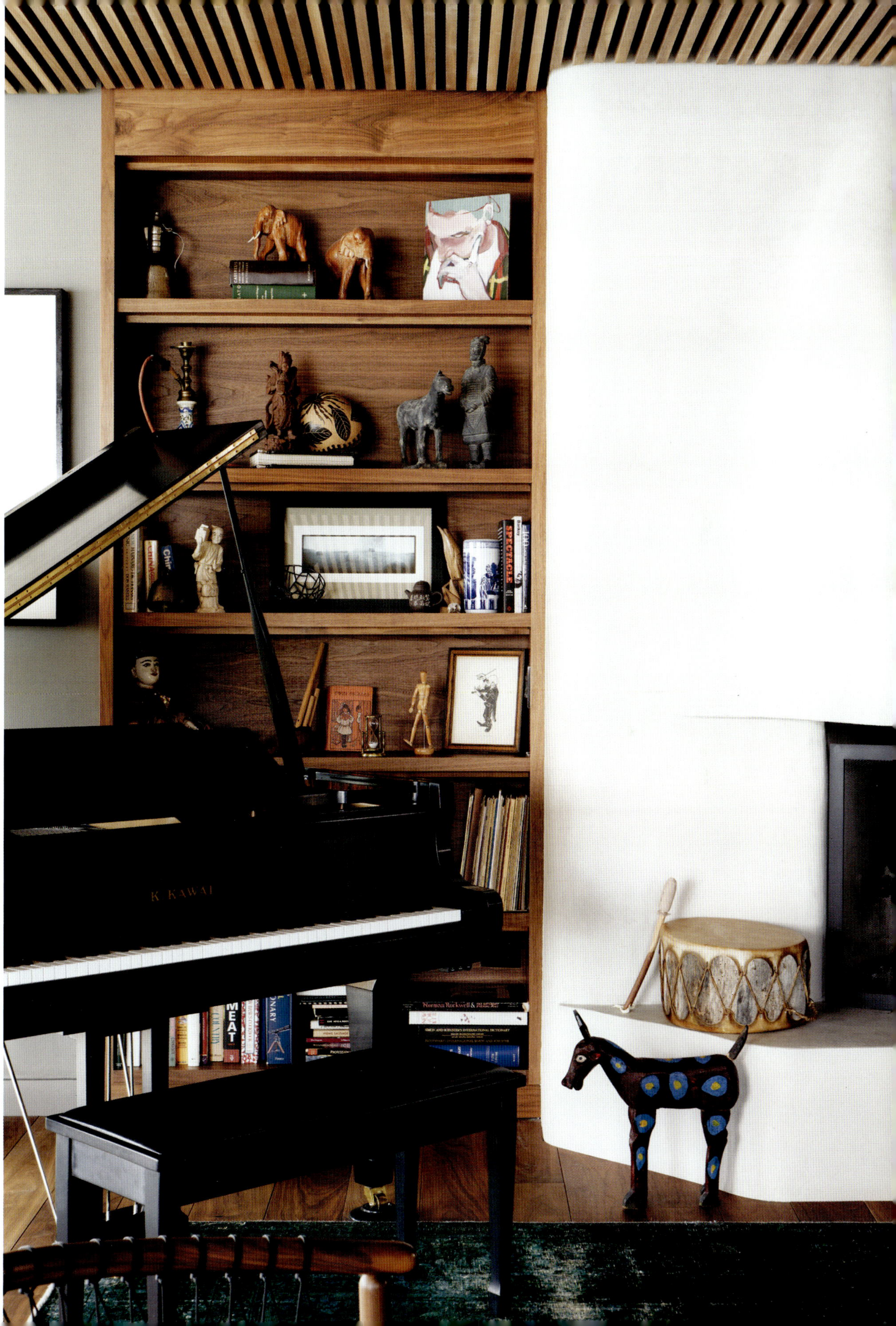

Profile: Two Tastemakers Tell All

We all have a love/hate relationship with social media, but tastemakers like creative director Benjamin Reynaert and designer Carly Cushnie have embraced it as a creative outlet for their personal style and professional pursuits. Collectors in their own right, both Carly and Benjamin seamlessly blend their collections, their homes, and their personal styles both in life and online.

Benjamin runs his creative agency, Benjamin Reynaert Creative, as an evolution of the community and aesthetic he originally developed on Instagram. His aesthetic is richly textured and one that reveals his affinity for thrifting and collecting. "Vintage and antique items that have had multiple lives and traveled across the globe speak to me. I personally could not live in a white box or a minimal space.

Objects that represent a moment of discovery for you and your style…evoke a true sense of home.

"There's a nostalgic element that comes through, and those textured layers are, to me, what great design and decorating is all about. It's really about pushing the envelope a little bit, trying something new and creating emotion. Especially when it's something that's not really done, rather than emulating something you've seen, you're having a dialogue with your own style."

1–3 Benjamin Reynaert uses his home as his styling playground, displaying his collections in different settings. Plates on walls, porcelain framed in built-in shelves, and a gallery wall showcasing his creative process—all change, move, and are swapped out on a regular basis.

1

2

3

115

4

5

6

116

4–6 Designer Carly Cushnie collects ceramics and glassware, many of which come from her travels. "It was probably my love affair first, but definitely something that my husband appreciates, too. Especially because I once made him carry a giant bowl (that I wanted to bring home) all over Morocco."

Carly is known first and foremost as a fashion designer, recently making a foray into interiors and product. "I love jumping from one thing to another, and having my hands in a lot of different things. Interior design is new for me, but it has allowed me to be creative in a way that left me when I was in the churn of running my fashion business for fourteen years."

Carly's warmly elegant home features heavily in her online presence, but Carly didn't let the clipping pace of social media influence her design decisions. "Designing my own place ebbed and flowed but I didn't want to rush it. It's our home and I wanted to find pieces that I loved that we could live with a long time. Sometimes when you live in the space for a while, you realize what you need.

"My collection of glassware and ceramics started in tandem with my travels."

"My collection of glassware and ceramics started in tandem with my travels. I have pieces I've found in Mexico (where my husband is from), Morocco, and some of our favorite places around the world. But we also have gifted pieces: crystal from my mother-in-law and a set of vintage glassware from good friends when we were married. They told us, "Don't be precious with it—we want it to be used!"

COLLECTED THOUGHTS

Objects that have interesting stories or are meaningful to you because you found them in interesting places or objects that represent a moment of discovery for you and your style, these are the objects that evoke a true sense of home.

Profile: Leyden Lewis

1   "My art collection pushes me to uncomfortable places, but many of my pieces are tied directly to personal experiences," says designer Leyden Lewis. His living area celebrates pieces from his personal collection, including a large colorful work from the *Point of Content* series, by Jeremy Lawson; a piece from *The Breast/Chest Portrait Project*, by Clarity Haynes; and *Red Black Blue Green Yellow Dirty*, by Kyle Goen.

Leyden Lewis has known nothing but interior design and architecture as a profession. The son of Trinidadian immigrants started as a "guy Friday" when he was seventeen, running errands in the Decoration & Design Building in New York City in board shorts and a T-shirt. "They were all, like, 'What are you *wearing*?' But I didn't know! I was seventeen!"

Now known for his thoughtful, material-focused, and joyful interiors, Leyden has a hands-on practice centered around personal narratives.

"I work on translating my clients thoughts, feelings, and essence into a physical representation that is their home."

"My own collection is my way of working through issues in my life, my self-identity, my understanding of my own narrative. I personally connect to the work."

This is not a task he takes lightly, and his own home and collection reflect that. "My own collection is my way of working through issues in my life, my self-identity, my understanding of my own narrative. I personally connect to the work." He describes many of the pieces displayed in his home as "challenging." His "most important piece" is by his good friend artist Lyle Ashton Harris, from his *The Watering Hole* series—a full set of which was acquired by the Museum of Modern Art (MoMA) in 2013. The collages examine the vulnerability of young, Black, gay, male bodies using serial killer Jeffrey Dahmer's Black, Asian, and Latino victims as source material. "It's hard for me to look at," Leyden admits, "but it addresses a lot of issues I'm still dealing with. I easily could have been one of those boys. The piece makes me look at myself, who I'm attracted to, and who society tells me to be attracted to.

"I'm determined to learn what people are saying through their art, and [I] challenge myself to meet them there, bringing my own perspective to the table. When I'm able to reckon with challenging, dark, heavy work, it makes my job of discussing unquestionably beautiful and light work with my clients not only easier, but also more meaningful.

"I don't come from a ton of money. I don't come from *any* money. So, one of my major assets is that I come to it [design] from a pure place. I'm trying to keep an artistic frequency as my highest level of addressing a design problem. Then after that, let's have some fun."

And that's the thing, because Leyden is so fun. His inner light glows brightly. "I'm living in this period that if I don't contribute to the celebration of who I am and who we are as a Black community, then I'm hiding it. And I cannot do that. I am always trying to find new ways to participate in unveiling who we are and what our joy looks like."

2   Leyden Lewis feels an imperative to share the joy of the Black community with the world.

3   Leyden's collection includes a large tonal black painting, *BLK02, 2009*, by Ricardo Gonzalez, juxtaposed with a life-sized man in white by Martin Sjöberg. Also seen on this wall are pieces by Jack Pierson, Tyquane Wright, and Leyden's father, Lionel Lewis.

4   Peering down the hall is *The Watering Hole*, by Lyle Ashton Harris.

COLLECTED THOUGHTS

Meet artists where they are to truly understand them, and how their work moves you. "I'm determined to learn what people are saying through their art, and challenge myself to meet them there, bringing my own perspective to the table."

Leyden participates in collecting as self discovery, finding "new ways to participate in unveiling who you are, and what your joy looks like."

3

4

121

Profile: Jonathan Boyd

[1] Jonathan notes that he doesn't go for the rarest or most valuable when adding to his collection

When I first met Jonathan Boyd in Santa Fe, New Mexico, his frenetic energy almost knocked me over. A whirlwind tour through the woodshop where he made stunningly crafted furniture for his company, Boyd & Allister, led to a quick car ride to his small house, a one-bedroom jewel box that he gut renovated and fully furnished with pieces he made. Which then led to a fast tour of the larger house (also his) next door. Jonathan speed walked through the big house, pointing to this thing and that thing he'd made, pointing out a four-poster bed with a delicate lace canopy, both of which he'd also made. Next was an invitation to a home-cooked dinner that night (he was a private chef in a past life) with his partner, Nina. I declined, because, after meeting him, I genuinely needed a nap.

Conversely, getting to know Jonathan Boyd takes time, sporadic bursts of texts and conversation gradually revealing a personal history that spans multiple careers and an ambition fueled equally by his passions and his quirks.

And so, his expansive collection of rare cacti came as no surprise to me.

It started in the small retail space in the entrance of his old woodshop. Beautiful design items for sale were styled with cacti. "I've always liked cacti. I find them incredible. How inhospitable they are to humans and yet how beautiful they are in their austerity," Jonathan says.

Admiration exploded into a full-fledged obsession when two things happened: (1) He met a cacti collector in Santa Fe who introduced him to "the weird world" of finding and acquiring truly rare cacti. (2) He built out the courtyard (between his small house and his big house) into a terrace and greenhouse for his collection.

"I would be coming home from trips to Arizona and LA with a carload of cacti," Jonathan explains, "and I'd have to find places in my house to put them that got southern light. I quickly ran out of spaces that had enough exposure, so I started rotating them, but it just wasn't working. Once I built my greenhouse and had the space, then I was uninhibited. I went out and started actively seeking plants I really loved, and I managed to build and grow the

2

3

4

3. EARTH 124

2–3 This house was built (and renovated) entirely by hand. Jonathan's love of natural light is evident throughout the space.

4 Cacti, like most houseplants, benefit from ample sun. Jonathan rotates his around the house for general display, but also has a greenhouse, where they can thrive in private.

5 Jonathan Boyd's kitchen is an important room in his house: He was once a private chef and is opening a restaurant in Santa Fe called Goldtooth.

COLLECTED THOUGHTS

I grant you permission to follow your (heart) eyes. It's OK to be aesthetically driven in your collection. "I don't go for the rarest; I go for the ones that I find to be the most beautiful, and it takes me all over the place."

When you find a passion, collecting can be a self-soothing experience, an outlet and expression for your compulsions. It's healthy, I think.

If you decide to collect plants, be prepared for the work that goes into keeping them alive. "It's a lot. [You] have to water and prune them constantly."

collection that I wanted. I'm aesthetically driven by my collecting. I don't go for the rarest; I go for the ones that I find to be the most beautiful, and it takes me all over the place."

It's also unsurprising that Jonathan thrives on the rigorous work that goes into keeping these plants alive. "It's a lot. I have to water and prune them constantly. I propagate and sell them, which is also the fun of it." Jonathan escapes into his greenhouse for hours to take care of his plants.

When paired with his passion for making beautiful furniture and textiles by hand—"my favorite thing to knit is lace, which is ridiculous. Only hundred-year-old ladies knit lace"—the detail-driven work of keeping and propagating cacti seems to uncover a hidden truth about Jonathan. "I've found a way to channel my compulsive and frenetic energy into making—and collecting—beautiful objects."

5

Profile: Animal Kingdom

Interior designer Ghislaine Viñas is known for her colorful interiors that have the ability to transport you to another world. Her home and home studio are just what you would expect: a menagerie of exciting collections that hint at a creative genius that sees the world in a kaleidoscope of design.

"I am not a pet owner," declares Ghislaine. "But I love animals and I'm always the one in the city petting people's dogs in the elevator, and in the country I love staring out the window at the birds, chipmunks, squirrels, and deer. My husband, Jaime, thinks I'm nuts, but I can actually identify some squirrels and deer that come by often enough. Obviously there is nobody to prove me wrong so this may very well be my own little pastime. I find that creatures have so much personality and bring life to interiors.

Her home and home studio are just what you would expect: a menagerie of exciting collections

"I actually was unaware of the fact that I was drawn to creatures until we published a project and they titled the story 'Animal Kingdom.' I was kind of surprised, but then I looked around my own home and thought, OMG, it's like a Noah's Ark in here."

1-3 Interior designer Ghislaine Viñas groups her collection of animals by species, to help bring visual order. "I find that creatures have so much personality and bring life to interiors." A painting by Pasqualina Azzarello is a centerpiece among her menagerie.

COLLECTED THOUGHTS

Ghislaine's collection of animals is an expression of her sense of humor, her design sensibility, and her curiousity. Let your delight take over.

3. EARTH

1

2

3

127

2 A wild collection for a delicately styled entryway console. The trio of monkeys are from vintage dealers and flea markets. The designer/collectors note: "No work or personal trip abroad is complete without a flea market stop."
3 An adventurous (and fun) monkey-themed collection

3. EARTH 128

3

4

5

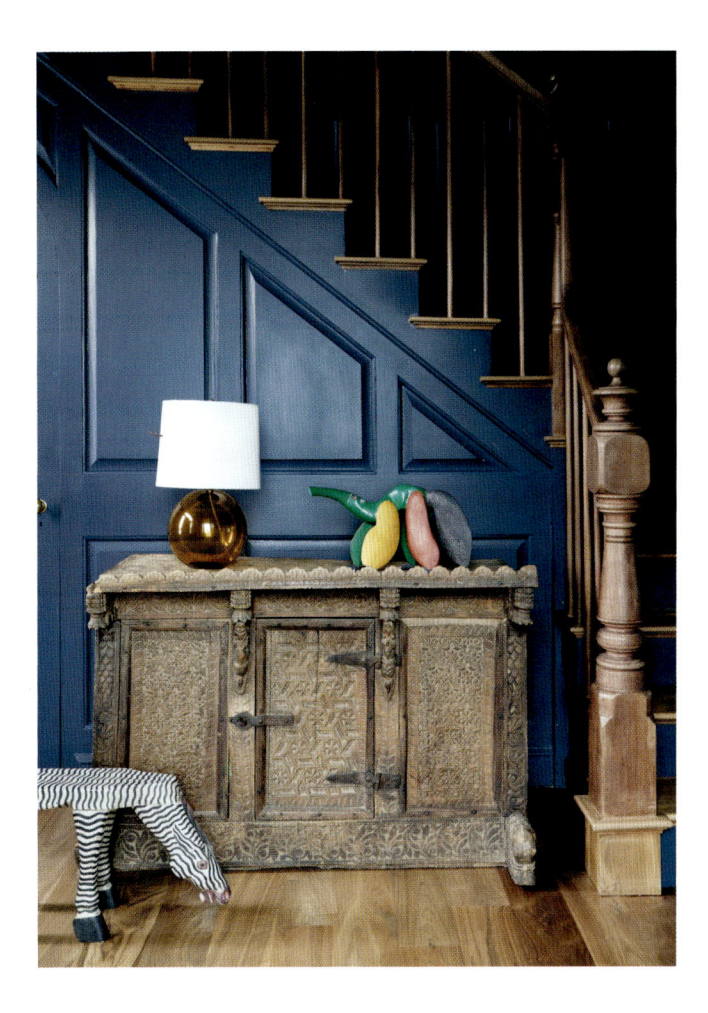

6

4 A vintage collection of taxidermy miniatures. Made from leftover scraps, the animals were designed originally as gifts for children.
5 A birdlike textile sculpture by artist Elodie Blanchard
6 A folk-art zebra and abstract elephant flank an antique Indian dowry chest and lighten the mood in the stairwell.

How to Collect Body Parts (a Guide)

- You don't have to choose just one body part, but if you do, choose one you *really* love.
- Artful over creepy.
- Creepy over cheesy.
- Materials matter:
- Bronze—always
- Rubber—sometimes, but maybe not for display
- Ceramic—yes, definitely
- Plastic—can we try not to?
- Display them in your home like hidden treasures to be discovered. Your parents won't even notice the vaginas everywhere if they're only in groups of two or three! And next to a plant!
- When in doubt, busts are always classy.
- Do I have to say it? No real body parts, please.

1. A collection of rubber vaginas on display at the home of Ghislaine Viñas.
2. Let's not question the purpose of these collected doll hands.
3. Busts are always classy.
4. Next to a brighly colored painting by Bethani Blake and chair, the monochrome grouping of wax bust, foot-shaped cup, and "dog" vase are (weirdly) not weird.

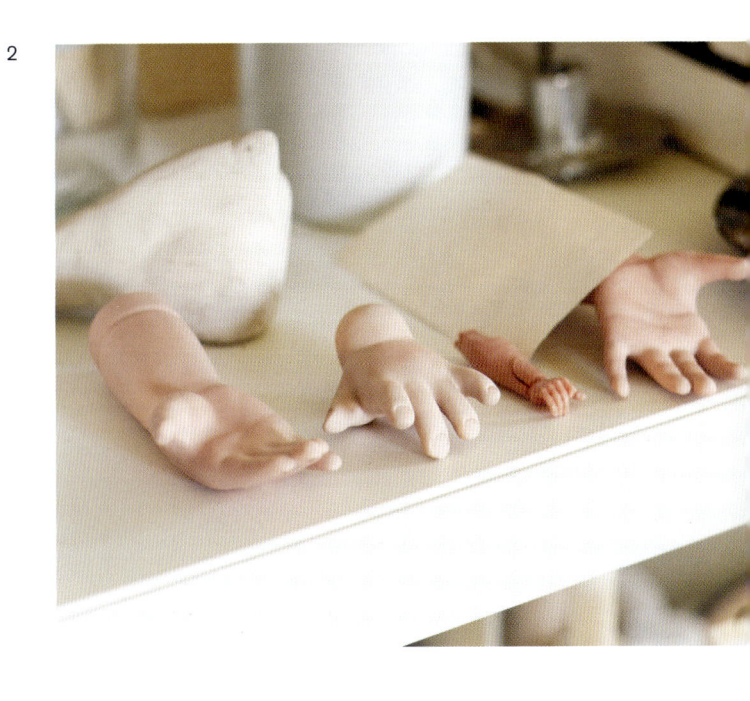

1

2

3

4

Profile: Maya Schindler

1   A peek down her hallway reveals the collector first, and upon further inspection you find that Maya Schindler is a design-lover.

2   Hand-carved candleholders cut a striking image against a white wall. When displaying such a collection, move things around and change the settings.

"I love entertaining, and they are a huge part of that," says Maya Schindler of her collection of wooden cutting boards. "They aren't artifacts; I use them all as serve ware." Maya is an Israeli-born artist and interior designer who sees her collections as utilitarian but also immensely meaningful and honest. Her upbringing in Israel was "complex," and as an adult she realized that she wanted to provide her two kids with physical mementos and heirlooms she felt were missing in her own life.

For a designer with a knack for collecting, Maya has a house that is refreshingly clear of clutter. Nicknamed the 6ft Up House, it manages to delight without overwhelming. No art hangs on the walls, she points out, because that feels so permanent, and her family likes to change and move and shuffle their favorite objects often. The cutting boards could one day be stacked tall and aslant as a centerpiece on the dining table, the next day leaned against a wall of the kitchen to dry. The quilt collection is stacked tall, a living barometer of how fast her kids are growing.

Each collection started with one item and eventually grew to "critical mass," she says of her cutting boards and quilts and blankets. Each piece has a meaning, a story behind it, and a use. Creating a new tradition of heirlooms for her family may seem like a tall order, but the kids get it. "They understand that someday these things will be theirs."

COLLECTED THOUGHTS

A collection can be useful and practical—but also meaningful and honest. Sometimes a collection can provide physical mementos and heirlooms that you felt were missing from your life before you became a collector.

3

4

5

3–4　Imperfection makes perfect: A tower of blankets in the living area and stacks of cutting boards in the kitchen tell the story of Maya's passion for travel and collecting.

5　Collections do not have to be behind glass: "Use everything," Maya advises.

6　Maya's home is beautiful but not precious. Everything is used and treasured in equal parts.

4.

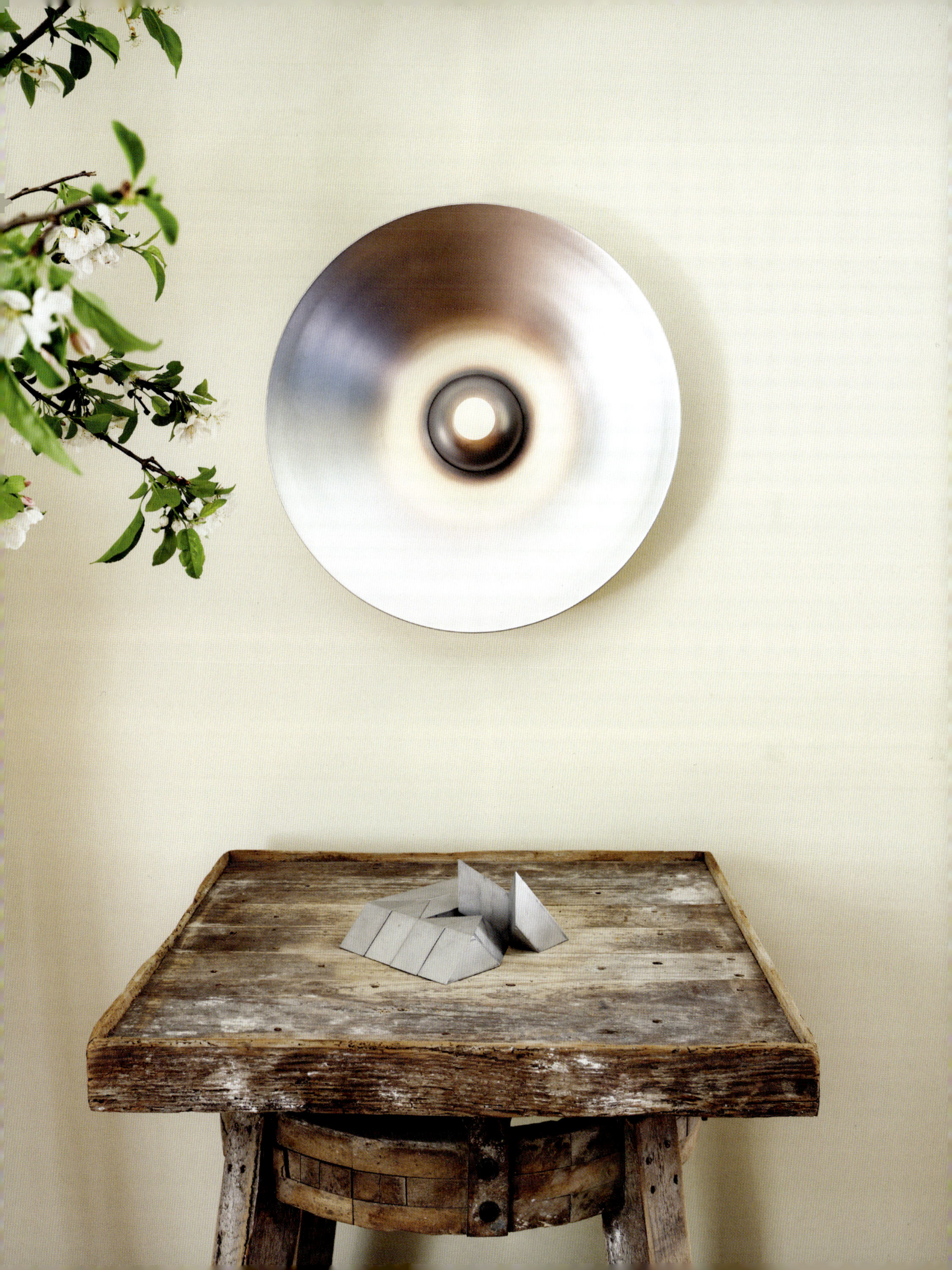

Metal

Metal, to many of us, can seem cold and unfeeling. But a special few know that, with a simple set of rules, metal becomes pliable, shaped to our will. This work requires discipline and adherence, a laborious science.

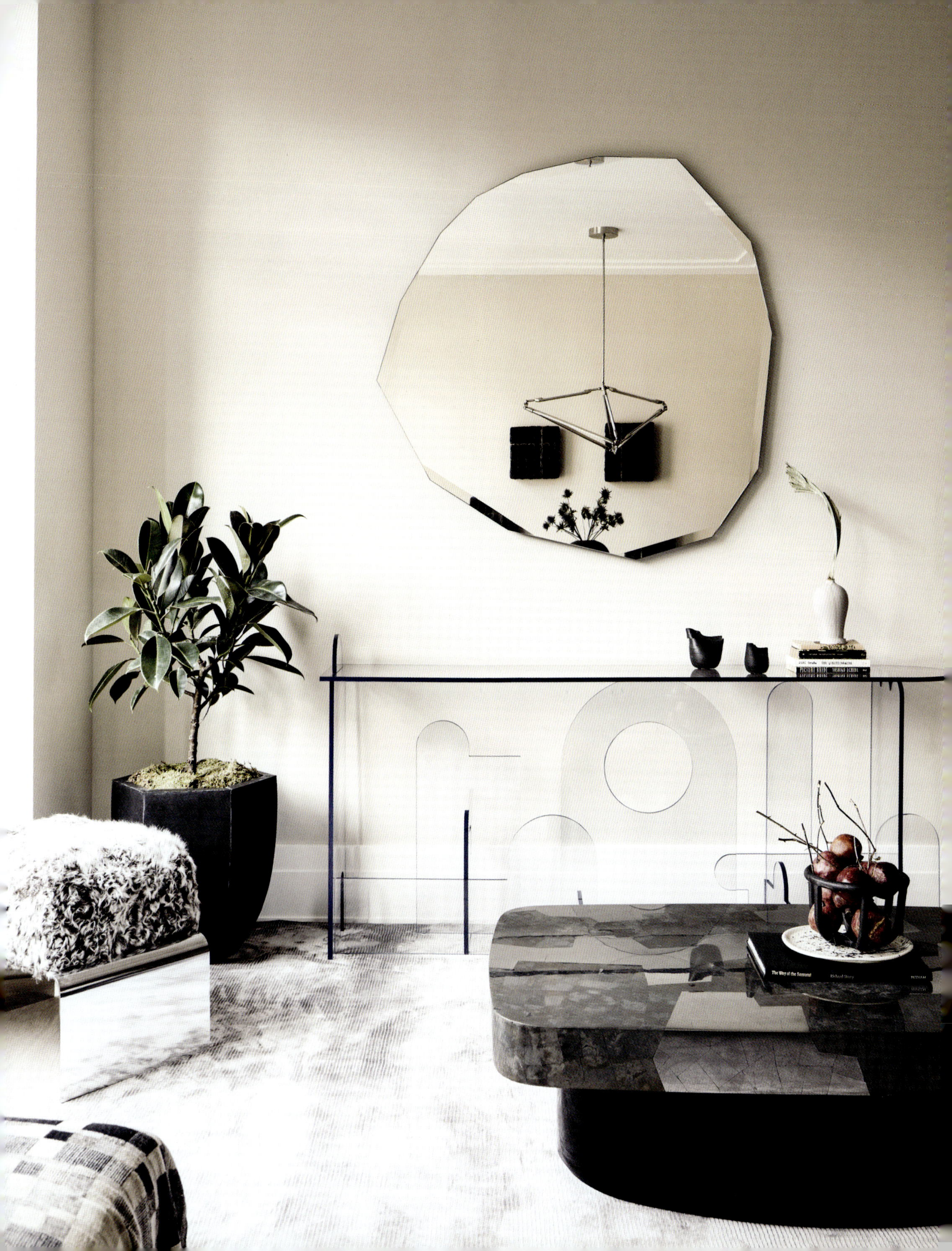
The Way of the Samurai
PUTNAM

1

1   These sterling silver trays are heirlooms from the collector's mother. Displayed on a stainless-steel bar cart, the grouping seamlessly marries traditional and contemporary sensibilities. A photograph by James Griffioen hangs above.

P. 138   Objects of interest by Carl Auböck

P. 139   The Monumental Sconce by Workstead

P. 141   Facet Mirror by Studio Paolo Ferrari, Lexan Console by Phaedo, Emil Coffee Table by Demuro Das

(See page 206 for additional information.)

The labor of forging metal starts to explain our relationship with it, its perceived permanence and its near-universal value. In the decorative arts, it has an everlasting appeal. Brass, bronze, and sterling silver are all calling cards of a well-appointed home. Beyond this, however, metal has revealed itself to me as a mentality: a structured approach toward creativity that depends on a certain set of rules to break free from form and become smoother or softer or playful or unexpected.

IN THIS SECTION:

144   A lighting designer's homestead
150   Sterling silver for dummies
152   The Four Carl Auböcks
156   Allyson and Julius, the structured approach of minimalist collectors
164   Art as toys, as collections and as charms to be found around the home.

Studio: Robert Highsmith

[1]

4. METAL

144

1 In designer Robert Highsmith's home studio, inspiring objects are put on display for tinkering—and gazing—while he mulls over new designs.

"I played violin starting at the age of five, and I have an intimate connection to objects from that point of view. I spent fifteen years of my childhood holding this beautiful wooden instrument every day. That definitely informed my interest in tactility, sound, and [even] buildings and everything in between."

Robert Highsmith started to feel limited by how temporal and fleeting his time as a musician was. "I would practice for days and weeks and months on end and then perform. But then it was gone, and I was on to the next thing." Searching for more permanence, he started exploring the visual arts and, eventually, architecture. With his now-wife Stephanie, Robert co-founded Workstead, the New York–based multidisciplinary studio known for interior design, architecture, and its lighting collection, of which Robert is the lead designer.

"My collection was started with inherited objects from my grandparents. They were modernist thinkers in the setting of the suburban South of the fifties. When I left for college, I took some of those objects with me, and it was a special way of starting my collection."

My collection was started with inherited objects from my grandparents.

When Robert and Stephanie purchased a historic New England house in western Connecticut, his collection expanded from those heirlooms in a meaningful way. The house, built in 1815, started to influence the pieces he was drawn to. "I have an ongoing fascination with the idea of folk modernism. The honesty of materials and the purity of the architecture of this house—and this era—in conversation with the wild yet formal landscape of New England has informed not only my collection but also the lighting [fixtures and lamps] I'm designing. Living here and building my collection has resulted in a very generative time for me.

"At Workstead, we have a throughline of a real attention to detail, a discipline and meticulous quality to how we do things and find beauty in necessity. We love to explore how the form of something can be celebrated in the way it functions.

"I've loved being in this space surrounded by all these objects, which I find have this embedded discipline. They speak to scale, shape, form, shadow, color, texture. There's so much intelligence in a single object. It's been enlightening to experience and respect some of these things from the past while also contemplating my own vision and how to create objects for the future."

2   An oddity, in this case the remnant of a windmill, becomes an artwork.

3   An unexpected twist of matching a lampshade to the wallpaper creates a delightful trompe l'oeil.

2

COLLECTED THOUGHTS

Family heirlooms are a wonderful way to spark passion for collecting. Understanding why something was important to your family brings a deeper understanding to objects with personal history.

4. METAL

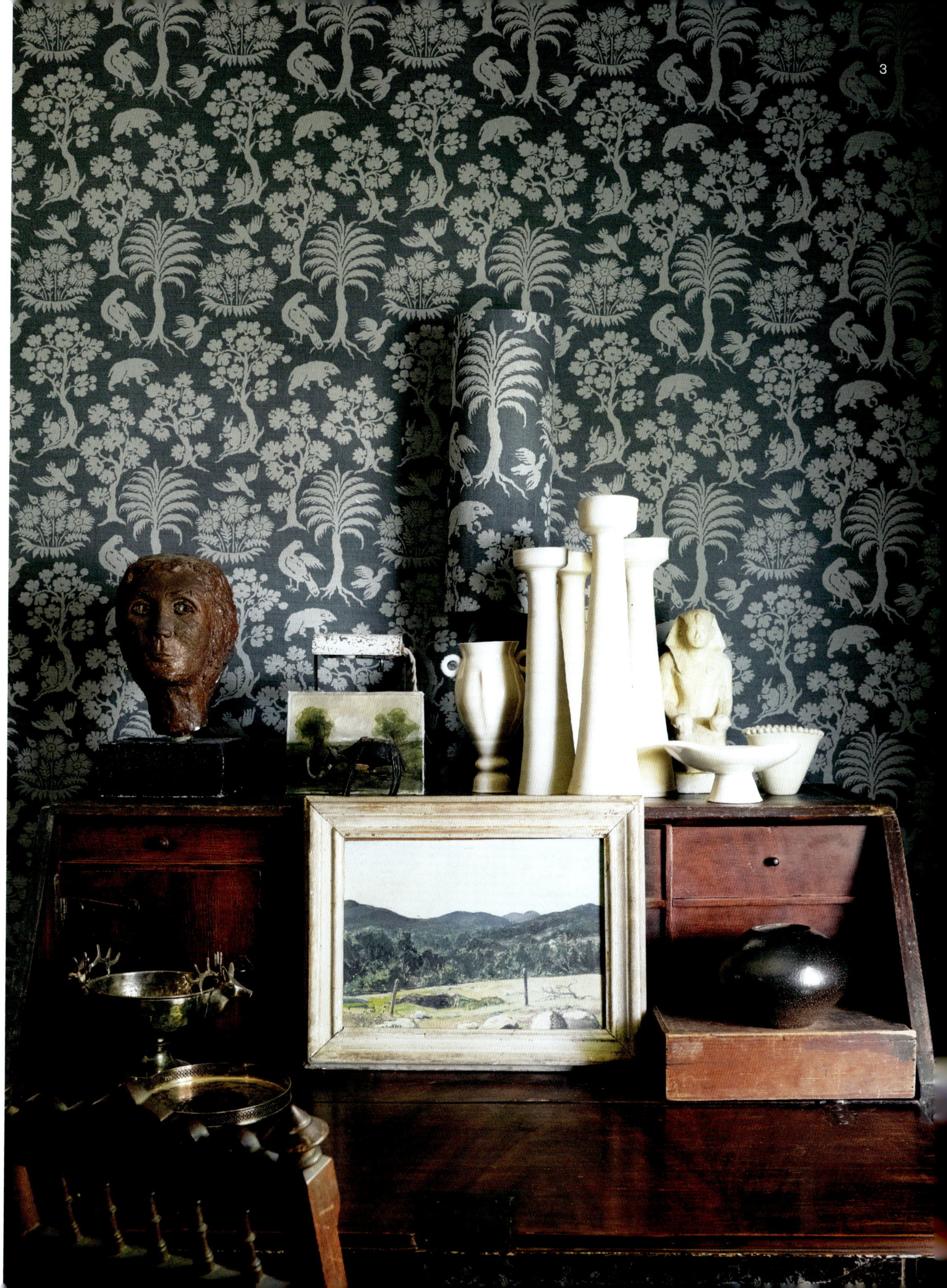

4. METAL

4   The renovation process changed very little in this historic home and focused instead on leaning into the existing elements of the dwelling.

5   Sunlight provides the perfect foil for new forms made in a familiar material.

6   Juxtaposition of scale: a smaller space, such as an entryway, is a perfect spot to show off monumental pieces.

7   Originally, this room's historic color was found only on the wall with the fireplace. Robert painted the whole room to match and placed his collection of vintage iron found objects on the mantel.

How to Collect Sterling Silver (For Beginners Like Me)

- Don't wait until you're retired. Sterling silver is cool, kids!
- Indigenous sterling silverwork is awe-inspiring. For a crash course, buy a ticket to New Mexico and go to Shiprock Santa Fe.
- Depending on whom you ask, antique English, Russian, and American sterling silver are all highly sought after.
- Find the maker's mark, which is the starting point for understanding where your silver came from (and how much it might be worth).
- Beware of silver plate masquerading as sterling; it's usually lighter in weight and not as lustrous in color as sterling. If you're purchasing online, you should ask for close-up images and a shot of the maker's mark to ensure that the piece is sterling and not silver plate.
- Keep an eye out! Sterling silver can be one of those collections where the fun is in the hunt. Finding inexpensive pieces at a thrift store or flea market is a rush.

1   A collector of silver teapots shares, "I enjoy looking at teapots from behind with their handles and tiny feet made visible. These are the small details that differentiate one from another. That's why they are lined up like soldiers with their backs turned. In the past, I used to reorganize them by replacing the ones I liked less with those I liked a little more. But now, I find each one to be unique on its own and an indispensable part of the entire collection. I think they all stand stronger together."

2   On display at Shiprock Santa Fe: Functional sterling silver treasures created (and then stamped with intricate patterns) by Indigenous artisans.

4. METAL

1

Profile: Collecting Auböcks

A TALE OF FOUR CARLS
There are four Carl Auböcks you should know about if you wish to embark on a collection.

Karl I founded Werkstätte Carl Auböck in the nineteenth century as a traditional metal workshop in Vienna, specializing in Viennese bronzes.

Carl II studied at the Bauhaus and apparently had a wicked sense of humor. He deviated from the traditional bronze figurines of his father and began making works that were at once sculptural, functional, and witty—pieces inspired by Bauhaus teachings and pieces that made the Werkstätte famous for modernist design. Particularly delightful and revered are Carl II's desktop tools and accessories. Both whimsical and precise, bottle openers shaped as fish, corkscrews shaped as giant keys, and paperweights shaped as cute little feet are just a few of the sought-after pieces from the mid-century.

Carl III was a trained architect and industrial designer, an eager and talented partner to his father for many years. His studies at MIT, where he met Ludwig Mies van der Rohe, Walter Gropius, and Ray and Charles Eames, inspired him to consider the United States a viable market for his family's catalog. It was Carl III who brought the Werkstätte into the international market, collaborating with labels such as Longchamp, Tiffany, Hermès, and Pierre Cardin.

Werkstätte Carl Auböck still operates out of its original Viennese town house. Led by Carl Auböck IV and his sister, Maria Auböck, both trained and practicing architects, the house still produces over 450 products and is one of the most beloved and sought-after names in the design world, thanks to the tireless efforts of four generations of Carl Auböcks.

1   Carl Auböck pieces, from corkscrews to letter openers to bottle openers (below), are favorites for designer and architect collectors hunting for mid-century curios.

1

2

3

2–3 "The provenance of an item is still thrilling to me," says the architect who owns this collection. "I still feel the thrill of the hunt." These fur-wrapped glasses, coin-turned bottle openers, and copper-and-wood pots are all Auböcks that stray from his more recognizable designs.

Profile: Allyson Rees and Julius Metoyer

4. METAL

[1] When they moved to their dream house, Julius and Allyson whittled their collections to the bare necessities, including Julius's cameras, which mark his evolution from amateur photographer to professional director.

Allyson Rees and Julius Metoyer have moved a lot in their life together. Not small moves, either: The two have crisscrossed the country from LA to Manhattan to San Francisco and then back to LA. "We've moved so much that we've whittled our stuff down and down and down and down. When you're in your twenties and you move, you just can't take everything with you. We had stuff that we liked, but we would edit every single time we moved," Allyson says.

"The small collections we do keep when moving has forced us to edit out possessions, and are the treasured exceptions."

"The small collections we do keep when moving has forced us to edit out possessions, and are the treasured exceptions. A mid-century Danish wall unit from my childhood home came from my grandmother's bedroom, so it holds sentimental value for me. I think it was even in my family's house when they first emigrated from Germany in the 1950s. When we moved here, my friend Fabi used it in her LA apartment for a few years, and when she moved to San Francisco, she asked to buy it from me. I did sell it to her, but we have an agreement that if I want it back, she'll sell it back to me.

"When you buy or inherit pieces of quality, they last," continues Allyson. And the beauty of Allyson's arrangement with her friend Fabi is good advice for all collectors: "Do we expect any of that stuff back? No, but we know it isn't gone forever."

Julius adds, "This was the rhythm we were in, editing down our pieces to only what we needed with each move. But that was all amplified when we bought this house."

And what of *this house*? You see, Allyson, a consumer-trend forecaster, and Julius, a director and cinematographer, own a house designed by preeminent modernist architect

Richard Neutra—an architect's architect whose works are on historic-preservation lists, celebrated as Southern Californian icons. When a Neutra home comes on the market, architecture aficionados of the Southern California ilk—read, Hollywood—come knocking.

"We are so, so lucky," says Julius of how they came to own a piece of architectural history. A friend and colleague, and the previous owner of the house, had toured Julius through just as he and Allyson were starting on their search to buy a place. "The feeling of walking onto the property and down to the house, it was incredible. There was a feeling of peace, and I knew that this was our dream house."

But the dream seemed so out of reach, and the place wasn't really for sale. The owner, a collector himself, collects *architecture*. With a staggering amount of iconic real estate in his portfolio, the Neutra house wasn't where he lived. He kept the design in its original intention and the house was used much more as a personal architectural museum, like Phillip Johnson's Glass House, but closed to the public.

"We were looking for a long time, and because we're so picky, we just weren't finding it. This man, my friend, knew we were struggling in our search, and at the same time he was interested in buying a property on the East Coast to add to his collection. The timing was both laboriously long and instantaneous, and he offered to sell us the house at a price we could afford. I can't stress enough how lucky we are.

"I mean, if he had put it on the open market . . ." Julius's voice trails off. "There would have been no way."

The couple was visiting Allyson's family in Vermont when the deal was finalized. Allyson retells the course of events at a clipping pace: "We were in Vermont when we found out the deal went through. We were out and about with my sister. We went to a bar and had champagne. Julius said, 'This is crazy. Let's go for a walk to talk about everything.' We went for a walk, and he proposed."

2   In masterful Neutra form, an entire wall of the house is glass in order to let the outside in.

3   A favorite quilt and reupholstered banquette are small touches that bring in color and warmth, while staying true to the architectural design.

4   Julius sees the cameras as "a representation of how my personal aesthetic has shifted over the years. They all have little stories."

2

3

4

159

5

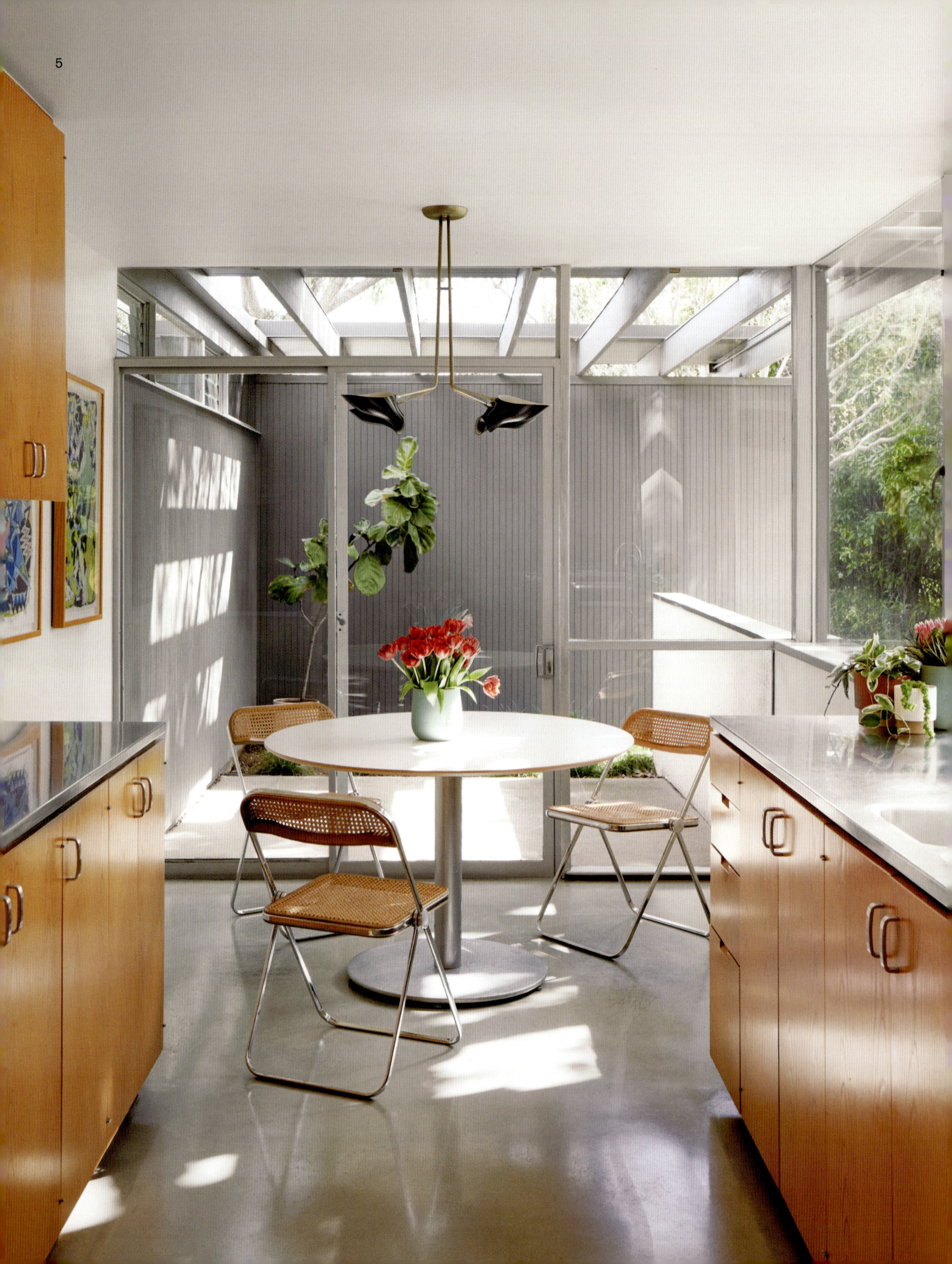

6

5   In Neutra's designs, dappled light is a planned and purposeful texture.
6   A small but growing collection of books about Neutra are a daily reminder of the history and architectural relevance of Allyson and Julius's home.

7

8

4. METAL

162

7   Allyson and Julius have sold or given away almost all of their furniture because their house has so much built in. These chairs and table are among the only pieces of moveable furniture in the house.

8   The dining table that Julius and Allyson kept from their previous home. "This house rejects furniture and art," says Julius. "We have to choose carefully and when we've chosen wrong, the house lets us know immediately."

COLLECTED THOUGHTS

Your collection has more personal value when you've chosen each piece, over and over, whittling down your possessions to the items you treasure most.

A collection isn't defined by possession or ownership when you have a like-minded community you trust. When you buy and inherit pieces of quality, you can use them, then give them away and they last. You don't expect that stuff back, but you know it isn't gone forever.

Collections can tell the story of the evolution of your style over time: Each piece has a story and shows how your aesthetic has shifted over the years.

"It's crazy, because that was planned," says Julius about the proposal. "Finding out we were going to get the house was *not* part of the plan."

The owner, the friend, the architecture collector, knew that Julius and Allyson would not only cherish the property, but that they would preserve the design in a way that would not betray its original intent. Much as with Allyson's furniture, he sold it to friends who he knew would take care of it. And they would sell it back to him if they ever no longer needed it. "We have a deal with him that if we want to sell it, we will go to him first."

Allyson and Julius's home is unique in that almost all of its furniture is built into the architecture. A built-in banquette acts as a sofa, the beds in each of the three bedrooms are built-in platforms, and open shelves and low cabinets provide storage. This is also why the couple's rhythm of letting furniture go was amplified when they moved in.

One collection that they've held on to is Julius's cameras. These cameras tell the story of the evolution of his style as a director. "I look at them as a representation of how my personal aesthetic has shifted over the years. They all have little stories: 'When I was seventeen I was into *this* style,' or 'I got *that* lens for my twenty-first birthday.' They are really personal to me in that sense.

"Most of my photos now are of my family, mainly my wife and my son. When I was younger, taking pictures of the world around me was my sole creative outlet. Even obsession. I would walk around cities for hours just shooting, listening to music, and being by myself.

"I don't really have time to wander like that anymore. I also think the world has shifted; people are so much more aware of photographers and even skeptical of having people with cameras around. Wandering with a camera just doesn't quite feel the same as it used to."

How to Collect Dunnies

"We were living on Bond Street when Kidrobot opened. I was very charmed by the play of it all," says interior designer Christine Gachot about the collectible "art toy" the Dunny, an anonymously bunny-like figure by Kidrobot and artist Tristan Eaton. Dunnies are released in limited editions, all designed and adorned by artists and designers ranging from famous graffiti artists to acclaimed fashion designers. Christine was first introduced to Dunnies when she was working for the developer behind the Standard Hotels, who collaborated with Kidrobot on a "Hello My Name Is" Dunny that has since landed itself in the MoMA permanent collection.

"The accessibility was always interesting to me. When they started, they were working with artists who were very of the moment and cool. But it was affordable artwork that you could actually collect in a significant way. It was something you could have that was designed by an artist you admired, and I loved that. It's incredible to me to see people of all walks of life, of all ages, and of all income brackets being so attracted to these characters. There's a democracy about these types of collectibles that really resonates with me.

"The kids got into it. I always loved the idea of collecting things that I could use to include my boys in the discussion. Their friends were part of the conversation, too, and there was this cool factor, like, their mom did that.

"They're not all displayed together—we have far too many. But they are meant to be more like charms, sprinkled throughout our lives and our home. They make us smile, and there are memories attached to them. They're little reminders for us all that art is important, and it can come in unexpected places. You always have to be on the lookout for it."

1–3   Built-in benches line much of the living area, including next to the fireplace; upon a high mantel, Christine found a home for two of the hundreds of Dunnies in her idiosyncratic collection. Benches, mantels, and a stack of books all work to display this collection, shelves optional.

COLLECTED THOUGHTS

The emotional value of a collection can oftentimes eclipse monetary or functional value of a collection.

4. METAL

1

2

3

165

5.

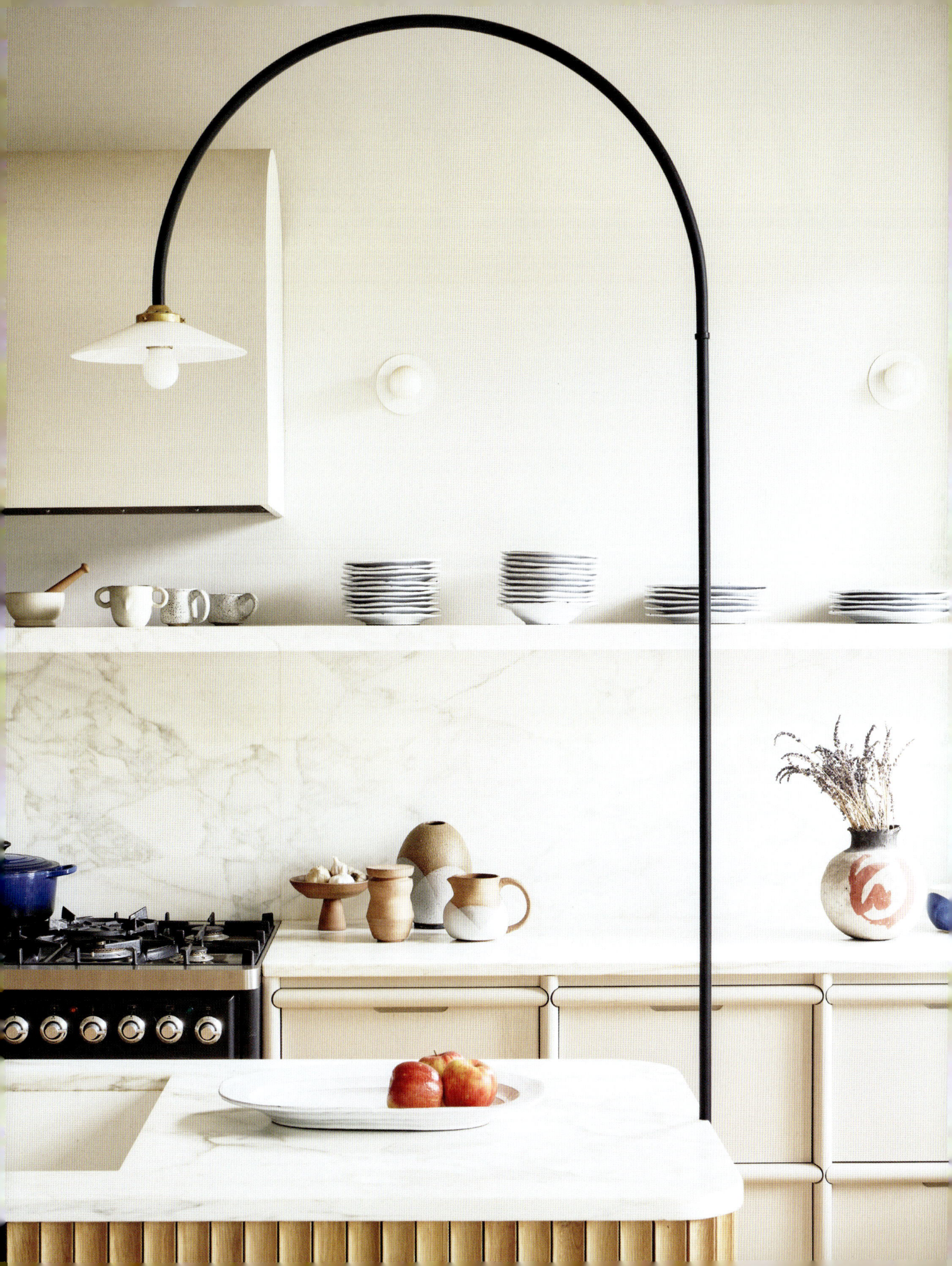

Water

At a Japanese *onsen*, you disrobe, and you sit at a shower head, and you wash. You wash your entire body: You wash your hair, you wash your face, you wash your feet. And as you wash, you are not only cleansed, you also find balance and clarity in the ritual.

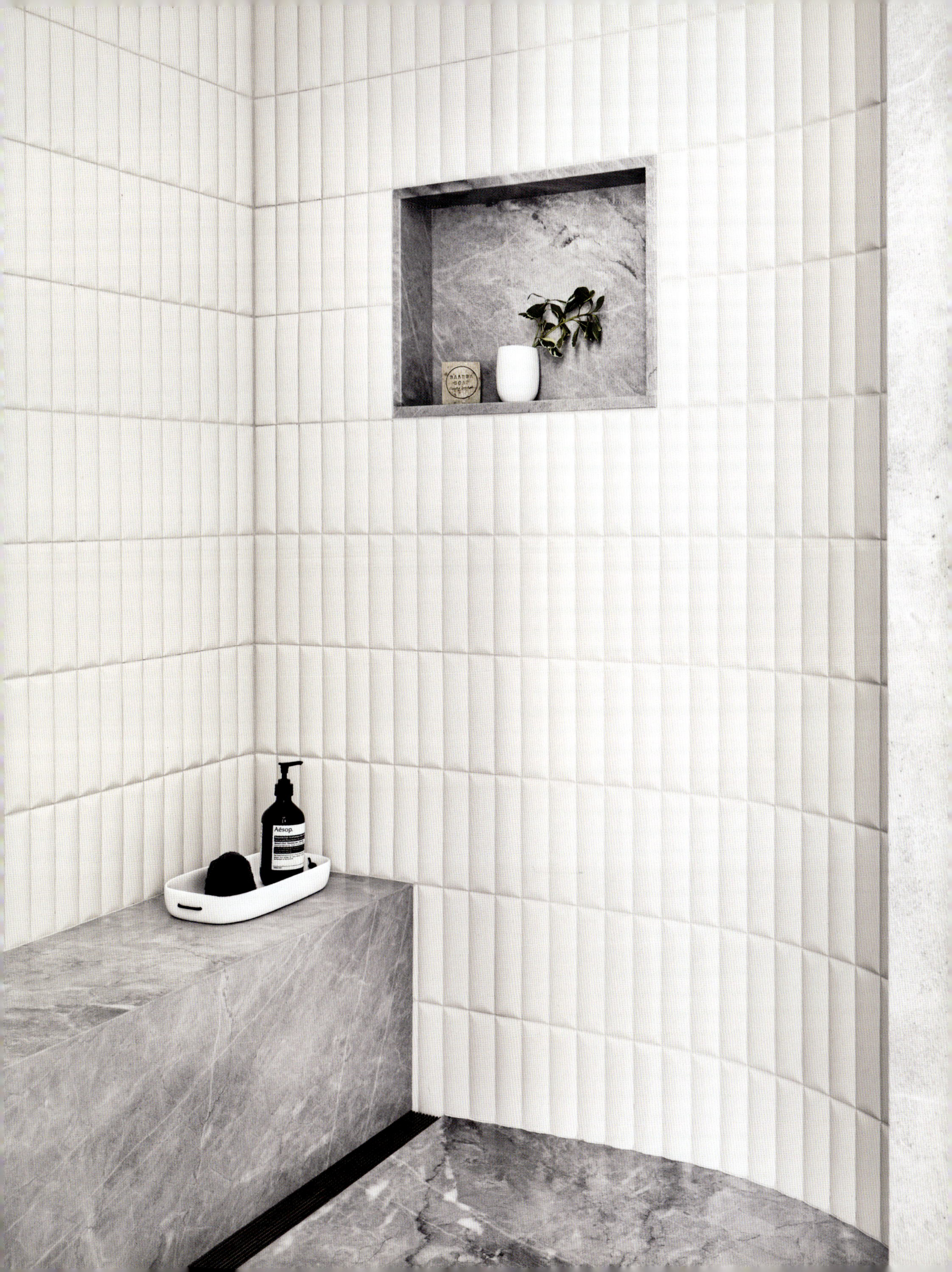
Aēsop.

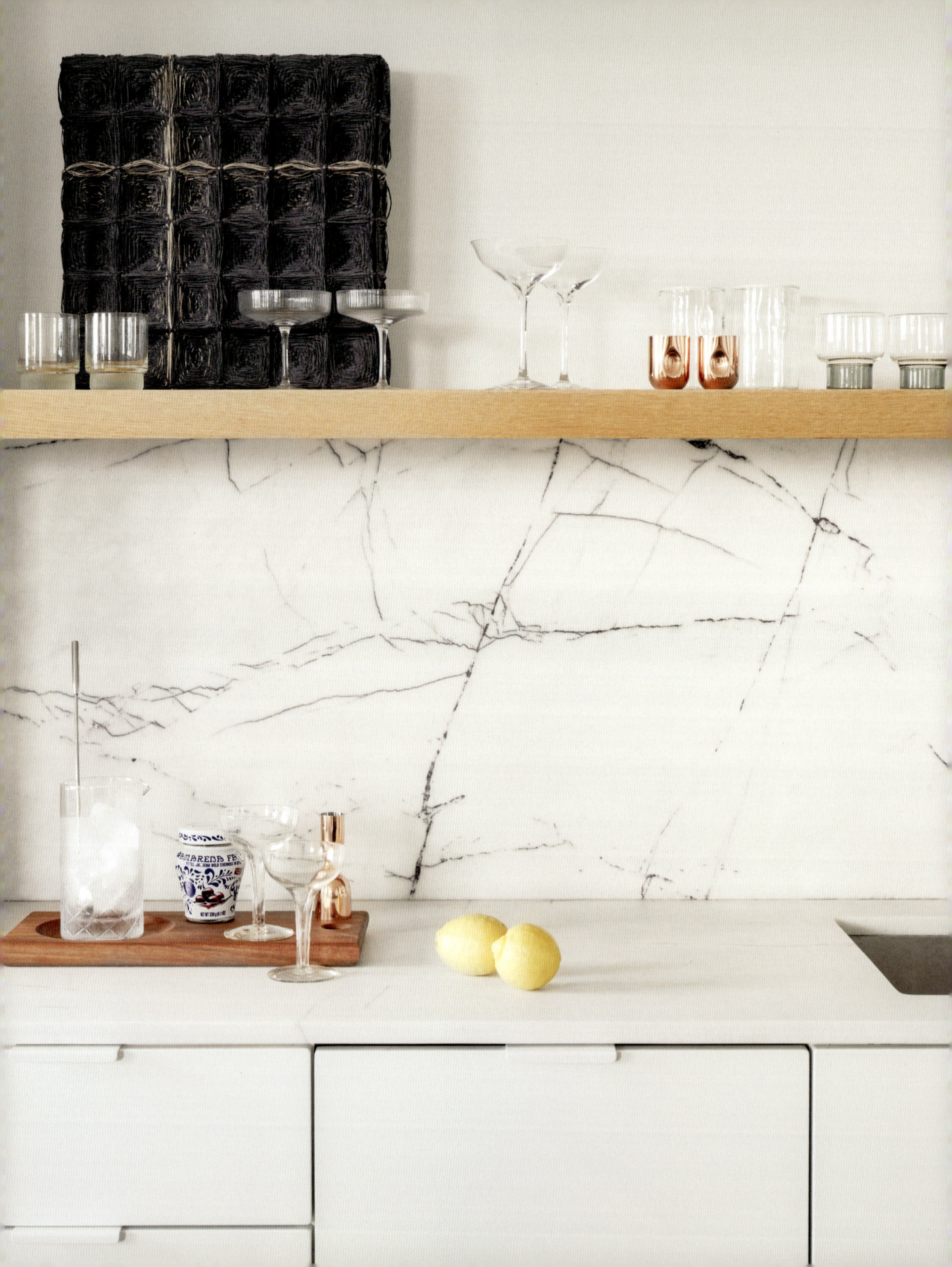

1   Pairs of cocktail glasses from Worrell Yeung's collection are highlighted by a weaving by Hiroko Takeda.

P. 166–7
   The flow of this bathroom and kitchen (both designed by Shapeless Studio) highlights a collection of busts and ceramics.

P. 169
   A shower designed by Worrell Yeung

   (See page 206 for additional information.)

You forget who is sitting to your left and to your right, but there is a peace in knowing that they are also washing.

When you finish washing, you enter the baths, hot springs naturally heated from the core of the earth, rich in minerals, and steeped in tradition. Again you realize you are not alone; in fact, you are surrounded by others who have come in search of all that the elements—wood, fire, earth, metal, and water—can provide. You enter the spring, and you are there, together with strangers and friends alike, bathing as one in the water of the earth.

IN THIS SECTION:

172   Worrell Yeung drink, collect, and live as a pair, but their work transcends the duo.
176   Collecting in the kitchen
178   Circular flow
180   The Tides of Family: Aleishall Girard Maxon and her grandfather's legacy
188   A collection born in Lima, Peru, travels over land and sea to New York City.
192   Aqua pura hospitality, the art of sharing space
194   Finding the source: Phillip Collins tells untold stories with Good Black Art.

Profile: Worrell Yeung

[1] Jejon and Max entertain in their kitchen often, but guests must use mismatched cocktail glasses. Their collection contains only pairs.

There's an unorthodox balance in Worrell Yeung's architecture. True symmetry usually eludes it, and traditional warmth is traded for material clarity. But when you see or experience a space the firm has designed, you feel the balance that is achieved when rigor and passion meet.

Max Worrell and Jejon Yeung followed what can only be described in hindsight as predestined paths toward architecture. Max's father was an architect who delighted in Max's letting go of an early rebellion against the field and finally deciding to follow in his footsteps. Jejon was a talented young artist whose primary childhood activity was drawing in a corner of his mom's office. Her friend, a psychic, knew nothing about his artistic abilities but upon first meeting him said he'd be very successful and that he should be an architect. Who could say no to fate?

They met on the first day of school at Yale in the Master of Architecture program. Jejon made a half-assed cabinet as his first project in the woodshop, and Max thought to himself: "Great, I'm falling for the worst designer in the class." But he fell anyway, the two becoming each other's greatest confidant through school, moving to New York together after graduation, and tying the knot four years later.

They shared their lives and their passion for architecture this way for nine years, still each other's greatest confidant, discussing this thing as successful architecture and that thing as not. A shorthand of their criticism and appreciation for their craft developed over this period, a time when they were just two architects who were married to each other.

Here's the thing about Max and Jejon, a thing I know because they are my beloved friends. They are common in that they see and mourn the fragility of life, but they are extraordinary in that, within tragedy, they have the strength to find clarity and purpose. Max's dad died unexpectedly, and within a month, he quit his job and started Worrell Yeung, his and Jejon's "thing from scratch." Jejon followed suit a few years later.

If you go to dinner at Max and Jejon's place—you do want to go, because they are amazing cooks—you and their other guests likely won't be served aperitifs in matching glasses. They have an expansive collection of pairs of cocktail glasses, but nary a third in sight. They love entertaining and always include cocktails before dinner, but have never felt compelled to purchase, say, a set of four? The collection marches two by two, pair after pair, unbothered by the idea of more.

And Worrell Yeung *is* about the pair. A studio is rapidly growing around them, but they remain a pair, nonetheless. Max explains their process: "We move in tandem, not always in sync, sometimes chasing one or following the other, but always on the path together."

2   In Max Worrell and Jejon Yeung's kitchen, unique pairs of cocktail glasses line a shelf.

3   I discovered this collection when Jejon served me a cocktail in a different glass from his and Max's. "Why?" I asked. "I guess we only ever buy two," he answered.

COLLECTED THOUGHTS

Your collection is an opportunity to strengthen your bond with those you love, a beautiful representation of your life and work together.

5. WATER

2

3

Profile:
A Kitchen Collection

"Broadly speaking, I collect tabletop: glassware, ceramics, vases," says Palestinian American Dania Ahmad, founder of Good Word PR. "I have low, medium, and higher-end pieces. Some fun things from mass retailers that I've had for years but can't let go of because they always get the job done. I love that none of it really matches but somehow it works.

"A lot of pieces were gifted, and some of the most delicate, precious pieces were ones I splurged on for myself and my family. Most of the collection is contemporary, but I have some traditional pieces like one or two Palestinian ceramics, which I treasure.

"We don't have a lot of space, so most of the pieces are in the kitchen or on the dining table. We renovated the kitchen with color in mind. This deep teal color makes us so happy, but if we could have, I think we would have draped the entire kitchen in this insane marble. It looks like a watercolor painting, and I'm so inspired by the fact that it was just naturally created by the earth.

I love that none of it really matches but somehow it works.

"I also love having open shelves. This way we can see all the pieces from the collection and also have easy access to the dishes and glasses we use every day. It's actually amazing that I still have so many pieces, since I am not someone who typically hangs on to things. I love spring cleaning! The truth is, each piece makes me happy, and many have a story or are connected to a person or experience."

1   Dania

2   An open shelf houses functionally important pieces.

3   Dania Ahmad's family kitchen is a celebration of both color and her collection of tabletop design objects. Here, green and yellow glass vessels find a home among a wild green marble backsplash and counters.

COLLECTED THOUGHTS

Dania's collection was built over time, and without a clear intention. The value of the collection has grown in hindsight, when the realization of what she had amassed and why she loved each piece became clear.

5. WATER

1

2

3

How to Find the Flow

One time I asked my friend, who is very successful, how he did it.

He told me about The Flow.

"I used to try to force things, based on my ideas of how my life should go," he said.

"It was hard.

"But I learned about The Flow. It's about submitting to the flow of natural energy, being observant of how things are going, and letting them go that way. Letting go of the control and allowing the flow to guide you," he said.

"It's no longer a straight line. It's a curved, many times a circular, path; one end overlaps and flows with the other.

"It's not always easy," he said.

"But it's no longer so hard."

1–2 A room with flow is both centered and open. Punctuated by a basket collection, each piece in this space leads the eye of the viewer to the next object, creating a fascinating progression.

1

2

Profile: Aleishall Girard Maxon

1

5. WATER

1   Alexander Girard was a mid-century icon and champion of folk-art sensibilities. His granddaughter, Aleishall, created Girard Studio out of love and reverence for his legacy, while carving a path for herself as an artist and a designer.

In Santa Fe, New Mexico, there is a small but mighty museum—the Museum of International Folk Art—and in this museum is a large room filled with whimsical, rustic, intricate, and unendingly inspired folk art. Actually, the room is a wing: the Girard Wing, named after the iconic mid-century designer Alexander Girard, who designed the exhibit and part of whose staggering personal collection is permanently on view.

Instantly recognizable for his optimistic, color-forward designs, Mr. Girard is behind some of our most beloved fabrics and objects; he was a key player in the American mid-century aesthetic as the head of the textile division of Herman Miller, providing the color, texture, and graphics that adorned our most enduring, classic, furniture designs. Over his prolific career as a textile, interior, graphic, and object designer, Mr. Girard took inspiration from his expansive personal collection and created a modern folk-art vernacular that still resonates today.

Upon first glance, his designs seem simple—colorful shapes stacked, whimsical and smiling—but further inspection reveals a composure and depth that hints at a thoughtful, nuanced, and artful approach that is a hallmark of work that stays with us, deemed timeless. The reward for such mindfulness is longevity. And the punishment for such mindfulness is longevity, with work so recognizable, it becomes ubiquitous, work so loved, one becomes cavalier about it. This was the conundrum that Mr. Girard's grandchildren, Aleishall Girard Maxon and her brother, Kori Girard, were faced with.

"Girard Studio was created about ten years ago," says Aleishall. "Both out of desire and necessity. As my brother and I finished our studies and were beginning to work in the art and design world, we developed an interest in our grandfather's archive and legacy. It just made sense that we take it back into the family and work directly with our collaborators to steer the business in a direction we felt did justice to this incredible body of work."

Generations of designers and artists have been influenced by Mr. Girard's work while not directly seeking it out, and Aleishall counts herself among them. "I am very fortunate to have developed my artistic practice from a very young age before I really understood the legacy I am part of. There is no denying that I was heavily influenced by my surroundings growing up, including the collections, interiors, textiles, and objects of my grandparents, but I never saw my own output in comparison to those things.

"I have been stuck on the idea of 'overlap' for some time," says Aleishall. "I've explored it extensively in the mediums of collage and watercolor and lately have begun to work through this concept in textiles. For me, the theme of overlap encompasses so much of our human condition."

2   Stacks of Aleishall's textile collection sit next to and on top of a chair upholstered in her grandfather's fabric design.

3   Aleishall Girard Maxon

3

4

4   In the studio, a stacked textile collection also provides inspiration.

And yet. The overlap of overlap surprises even her. Recounting a discovery of unseen archival work, Aleishall found many of Mr. Girard's tissue paper collages, which he used as studies for his textiles. "At that time, I myself was in the midst of creating tissue paper collages, studying color, composition, and how the overlap of material could create shadow and depth. It took my breath away to find these pieces of my grandfather's. It was like looking at an old family photograph and recognizing your own face in that of an ancestor. But it was art."

"It used to be sort of a game, to find items I collected in random antique malls or flea markets."

Like her grandfather, Aleishall is a collector. This overlap, she knows, is in her DNA. "The impulse to collect is so strong," she says. But her evolution is apparent, even when considering her collections. "It used to be sort of a game, to find items I collected in random antique malls or flea markets, but over time the idea of collecting just to amass a number of similar objects has become less interesting, and I am more drawn to collecting things that bring positive energy into my home or studio. It could be the shape of a bowl, the pattern of a textile, or the color of faded vintage paper. I really want to create an overall landscape of objects that are in harmony. With each other and with me."

Her most precious collection is her textiles. "Even before I understood the incredible breadth of my grandfather's textile designs, I was surrounded by and interested in beautiful fabric. Pieces from my home and my grandparents' home made a strong impression on me, and, when I was growing up in Santa Fe, there was no shortage of beautiful textiles."

Aleishall explains her textile collection as vividly sensory. "I still remember the weight of the velvet broom skirt my mother gifted to me, the stiff, robust feeling of an old denim shirt I borrowed from her closet, and the crinkly texture of a seersucker comforter on my bed. I have collected textiles for many years, some because I couldn't stand to leave them behind, others because I saw an immediate use for them. I love to see my textiles in stacks around me for comfort and inspiration. My most recent works are quilts made from collected pieces of family and friends' clothing. Utilizing textiles that have been worn by those I love puts me in direct conversation with the energy, work, struggle, and triumph that these textiles have been party to."

When asked directly, and plainly, about the influence her grandfather's legacy has had on her own work, Aleishall is clear. "I must also emphasize that one of the strongest impressions left on me is the relationship between my grandfather and my grandmother. As I've learned more about their lives, it has become exceedingly clear that he could not have done half of what he did without her by his side. Her dedication, organization, style, and steadfast belief in his abilities has influenced me just as much as his design aesthetic.

"The strongest influence he had on me is how he saw the world. He never sat us down and said, 'This is how you design this, or you should consider this . . .' It was just being in his presence and seeing his work ethic."

And there it is, the family tree that has left an indelible mark on an industry, a world of design lovers, and Aleishall Girard Maxon, an artist who is fascinated with the aesthetics and meanings of overlap, the space we all inhabit together and that we each inhabit alone.

5	Alexander Girard working in his studio.
6	*Overlap No. 4* by Aleishall
7	Aleishall's grandparents

COLLECTED THOUGHTS

Paving your own way while respecting your history is a universal pursuit, whoever your family is. Understanding the creative power of collecting, however, seems to be a learned virtue.

5

6

7

Profile: Carlos Runcie Tanaka and James Tanaka

[1] The ceramic statue has a glass-and-steel base that Carlos designed as a memory box, in which to place items of personal importance.

Peru-based ceramicist and sculptor Carlos Runcie Tanaka and James Tanaka are cousins. James's childhood in Lima, Peru, was one of familial community—his relatives all lived nearby. The family would gather in the home of Carlos's mother, a space filled with treasures and art, including a bounty of Carlos's ceramic sculpture as well as functional pieces like mugs and dishware. It was a time James remembers with fondness and nostalgia, and now that he lives in New York City, his collection of Carlos's ceramics is rooted in these memories of his childhood. "For me, it's about re-creating the connection to a larger familial space. How do I tie myself back to my time in Lima? How do I re-create this feeling of a large and extended family?"

Carlos's work evokes Peru, both its natural landscape as well as its socio-political history. Much of his early work echoes pre-Hispanic Peruvian clay forms, conjuring relics, treasures from the distant past reinterpreted through a personal, contemporary lens. However, some of his most striking sculptural works, and the apex of James's collection, are large standing humanoid figures, all with different glazes, colors, and subtly different forms, but each in a similar stance—the slightest forward bend, hands tentatively outstretched. Carlos explains that the figures originally were representative of his family's coastal heritage. "The hands were symbolically holding crabs caught from the ocean."

Once a collector takes on a piece, it transforms again.

But in 1996 Carlos found new meaning in the work. While he was attending an event at the Japanese ambassador's residence in Lima, a group of guerilla militants called the Túpac Amaru Revolutionary Movement (MRTA) raided the home and held more than one hundred government officials and civilians—including Carlos—hostage, many for more than one hundred days. "While I was being held hostage, it occurred to me that my figures were also a symbol of honest, human communication. We are made of

2

2   An early work by Carlos sits on James's coffee table. "It was the first piece my parent's acquired, and I've always loved it and wanted it as my own."

3   The Tanaka family, circa 1970s

COLLECTED THOUGHTS

James longed for a feeling of home, and found it in collecting his cousin's work. His collection is one of nostalgia and building a new foundation of memories for his children.

A collection has the power to bring heritage, family, and personal history together and into the present.

the earth and the ocean and the elements, but without the ability to listen and be heard—the ability to be open to what other people need—we are nothing.

"After being released, I was determined to put together a show, one hundred of my figures to represent the hostages. It was a very painful time for me, my life and my art coming together, because even as I was exhibiting this piece, and people were relating it to this socio-political situation, there were still hostages inside the ambassador's residence."

James, on his collection: "It's been an incremental process. Every trip home for the last twenty-five years, we've come back with one or more pieces—often what Carlos was doing at the time. Once the collection reached a critical mass, we started working with Carlos on filling in the gaps. What are we missing to be able to tell the story? And the figures have been instrumental in that process and, consequently, our collection."

Carlos's work now defines the home that James shares with his husband, Dan, and their two young children. In reality, nowhere near "critical mass" but clearly thoughtful in curation, the pieces tie James's family to their roots in Peru.

"I'm so grateful for James and Dan's support of me and my work," Carlos says. "Their patronage has often come when I needed it the most. But I also appreciate the continued life they give to my pieces. Once a collector takes on a piece, it transforms again. I start with a lump of clay, and James takes it and stretches it and molds it into something new, something beyond myself."

3

How to Share a Space

- Don't neglect your entryway. First impressions never have a second chance.
- Prioritize conversation over television.
- Overestimate how many people will be in your space at once—extra seating in the form of ottomans, benches or stools will work wonders. Your guests can thank me later.
- Fuzzy seating always makes sense.
- Display your most prized collections loud and proud. Dining table, coffee table, bookcase, mantel—all are fair game for your favorites.
- If you don't want them all out at once, rotate pieces in and out of storage.

1   Vintage beer cans are a source of artful marketing inspiration for a collector and business owner.

2   Monochromatic ceramics, stairs, and molding create an ethereal entryway.

3   Three carefully selected ceramics, chosen from a collection of hundreds, welcome admiration from their perch on this mantel. Hanging above is a print by Mayumi Oda.

3

Profile: Phillip Collins, Good Black Art

1   Good Black Art was born in this loft. Phillip Collins, its founder and a former marketing executive, wanted to share the stories of the Black creative diaspora.

"Media puts out particular narratives about everybody. We *all* get comfortable with it. What Good Black Art does is use art as a communication tool to talk about the nuance and diversity and the beauty of *all* Black people that the media has never shown."

Some people have an inescapable magnetism about them. They have a focus or an openness or an intensity or a warmth that makes you want to cheer for them or work with them or marry them or be their best friend forever. Phillip Collins, the founder of the art platform Good Black Art, is one of those people. His business is one of those businesses, and his community of Black artists—they are the heartbeat that keeps it all going.

Phillip left his Southern roots after college, working for years in marketing overseas in Asia. He was happy on his rising star until he woke up one day and realized he had outgrown his gangbusters corporate marketing career and felt drawn to tell stories in his own voice, rather than for large companies. "I kind of grew out of it. I loved being there, but I thought: If I'm gonna be a marketer, if I'm gonna be a storyteller, I have to start doing it in my voice, and it has to be in a tone of voice that is authentic to me.

"My life really started to shift almost immediately after I returned to the United States. Almost immediately all the [nation's] racism, all the homophobia, all that came right up to the forefront [of my consciousness]. I had never dealt with any of that trauma, because I just kind of left. In China—of course there is racism there, too, but it was more out of a place of ignorance and lack of exposure than a place of hate. Here, there was this bad energy happening. It was my first time working in the [States]. It was the first time I was a Black man [here]. When I left, I was a kid. The reentry to this country in such a volatile time was extremely difficult for me. The racism was all-encompassing."

Phillip's collection started quietly and as a therapeutic practice to help him heal from the trauma of the racism and aggression he was experiencing in the country he called his own. "I was a little heartbroken. I always knew that creativity was the way that I pulled myself out of

2   The photograph *Untitled*, by Phillip Prince King, welcomes you into the kitchen.
3   A gallery wall of Good Black Art including works by, counterclockwise from bottom left, Adrian Armstrong, Steven B. Williams, Nancy Boy, Kvvadwo Obeng, Robert Peterson, Brandon Hicks, Anthony Peyton Young, Dimithry Victor, Mario Joyce, Brian Brigantti, Steven Mark Finley, Blake Gildaphish, Stéphane Gaboué, and Tae Ham.

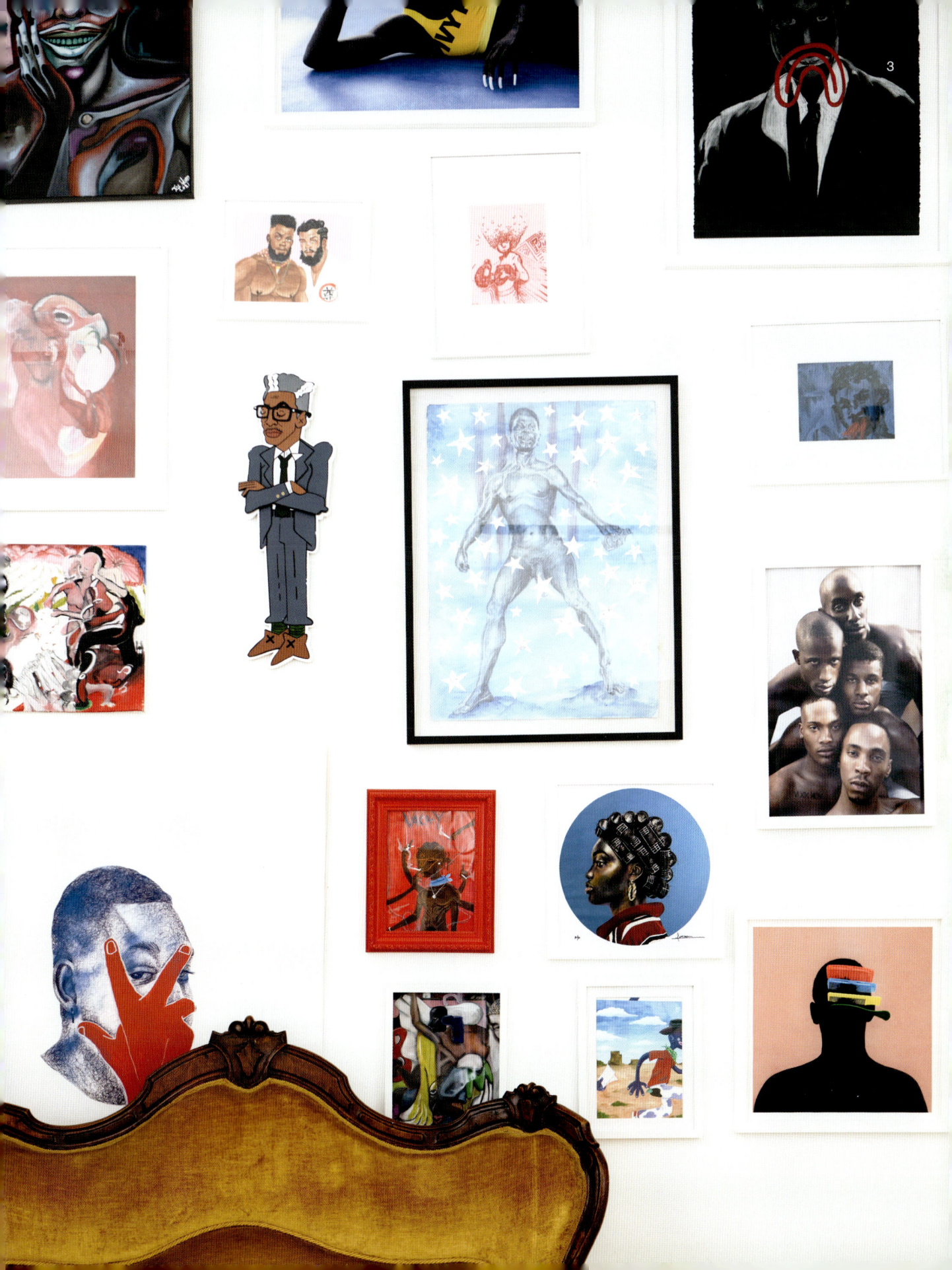

3

personal pain. Whether it was performing, whether it was making things, whether it was traveling, those were the tools that I had that helped me process trauma.

"So, I started just connecting to the Black art community. I started reaching out to artists, Black emerging artists from all over the world. I hadn't necessarily bought anything yet, but I was feeling it out and trying to understand it. And I realized that it was healing to look at work that reflected my personal experience. And even though I didn't have the words at that time to explain it, the artwork was a vessel of communication. It helped me build a whole new language to explain who I was. That was really special."

And his collection grew, as did his passion for connecting

And his collection grew, as did his passion for connecting with artists from the Black diaspora.

with artists from the Black diaspora. He was tenacious in his collecting, fully acknowledging the many barriers to entry into the art world for budding collectors (financial) and emerging artists (exposure) alike.

"I was watching a master class with Issa Rae, and she was talking about creating spaces. She said, if you have the resources to change a problem and you choose not to, then you're a part of the problem. If you don't see something [you want to see], you have to create it. It felt so specific and directed at me. I knew all the challenges in the art industry, I knew what emerging artists were going through, I knew what budding collectors were going through. I also knew that I had figured out a way to build a great collection despite all these circumstances. I was like, all right, this is probably what I need to be doing."

Phillip sees that the answer to both sides of the coin involves providing knowledge, access, and mentorship, changing the status quo of the art industry. "One of my

4   Phillip's communal home is a supportive space for the narrative around Black artists.

4

5. WATER

5   Phillip Collins occupies the role of both collector and champion as the founder of Good Black Art.

biggest challenges with Good Black Art is that the model in art perpetuates the same stories and narratives that the media repeatedly tell. Even if the stories are nuanced and the work is coming from a nuanced place, the model to sell is still exactly the same. You send out the preview, you sell the work, and repeat. There's no time for context, and there's no time for dialogue. There's no time to ask questions like, where and what mindset was the artist in during that time? Where are they from, what experiences molded them and their approach? Instead, the questions are: How much? Is it available? Will it appreciate?

"I'm not saying that those questions aren't valid, but at Good Black Art, we're trying to balance and, honestly, tip the scales. I believe that if there's context and conversation and depth, people fall in love with works. They fall in love with artists. The pieces will naturally sell. It just takes more time and energy.

"Through Good Black Art, I'm just a facilitator. And I love it, because I get to learn, too. I get to learn every single day about the amazing breadth and diversity and beauty and resilience and tenacity and intelligence of people around the world who look like me. I didn't have that growing up in northeast Tennessee. I didn't have a road map to get here.

"So, for me to be able to say to emerging artists, OK, here are all the tools that you need, go for it and tell your story, it just accelerates their growth. But I think on a macro level it accelerates all of our growth. My ultimate goal is to use Good Black Art to help these beautiful individuals impact the communal whole."

COLLECTED THOUGHTS

Collecting can be a tool for healing and for opening our understanding of self and of what we can offer to our community.

Before You Go

After a good party—the magical kind, where you're sweaty before you realize you're hot, where faces are alternatively familiar and a blur, where you don't have to shout but it's not for one second quiet—after a party like that, the very best part is the calm after everyone's left. It's just you and your bests, exhausted and smelly, half-heartedly cleaning up but joyfully recounting this thing and that in raspy voices that sound unfamiliar in the recently emptied room.

Colony has had many of these parties over the years. Nowadays, the team enjoys those moments without me; I've left when my son, Juno, decides he's had enough. For many, many years, it was me and Madeleine, my number one gal, ignoring the sticky floors (we would mop in the morning) and, instead, gossiping about our favorite designer who hooked up in the stairwell.

But in the very early days, it was just me in the quiet. Marveling at how many people had come. In awe of how beautiful my gallery looked in the still of the middle of the night. At once unbelieving and proud that a line had formed down the block of people waiting to get in and see the work. In those moments, early in my business, the bass of my pounding heart had echoed off works of design and art so beautiful, I had never dared dream them until that night.

It was in that midnight echo where I came to fully understand that beauty has nothing more important to give than the spirit of the people who create it. That is the spirit I hope has been captured within the pages of this book.

A daughter can honor her father's legacy by continuing to make furniture so beautiful that it represents the lineage from tree to hand to home.

A ceramicist can examine the depth of her cultural identity through her pots shaped like food.

An architect can find the maker of his obsession in a far-flung place that somehow feels like home.

A couple can find their calling in each other, with each other, and impossible otherwise.

My hope is that this book is a testament that the stories of what we keep, and why we keep them, are worth telling. Because it's in the telling, and retelling, that we can find ourselves and one another in a universal understanding: The beautiful life is not only to be pursued alone, but also uncovered together as a collective.

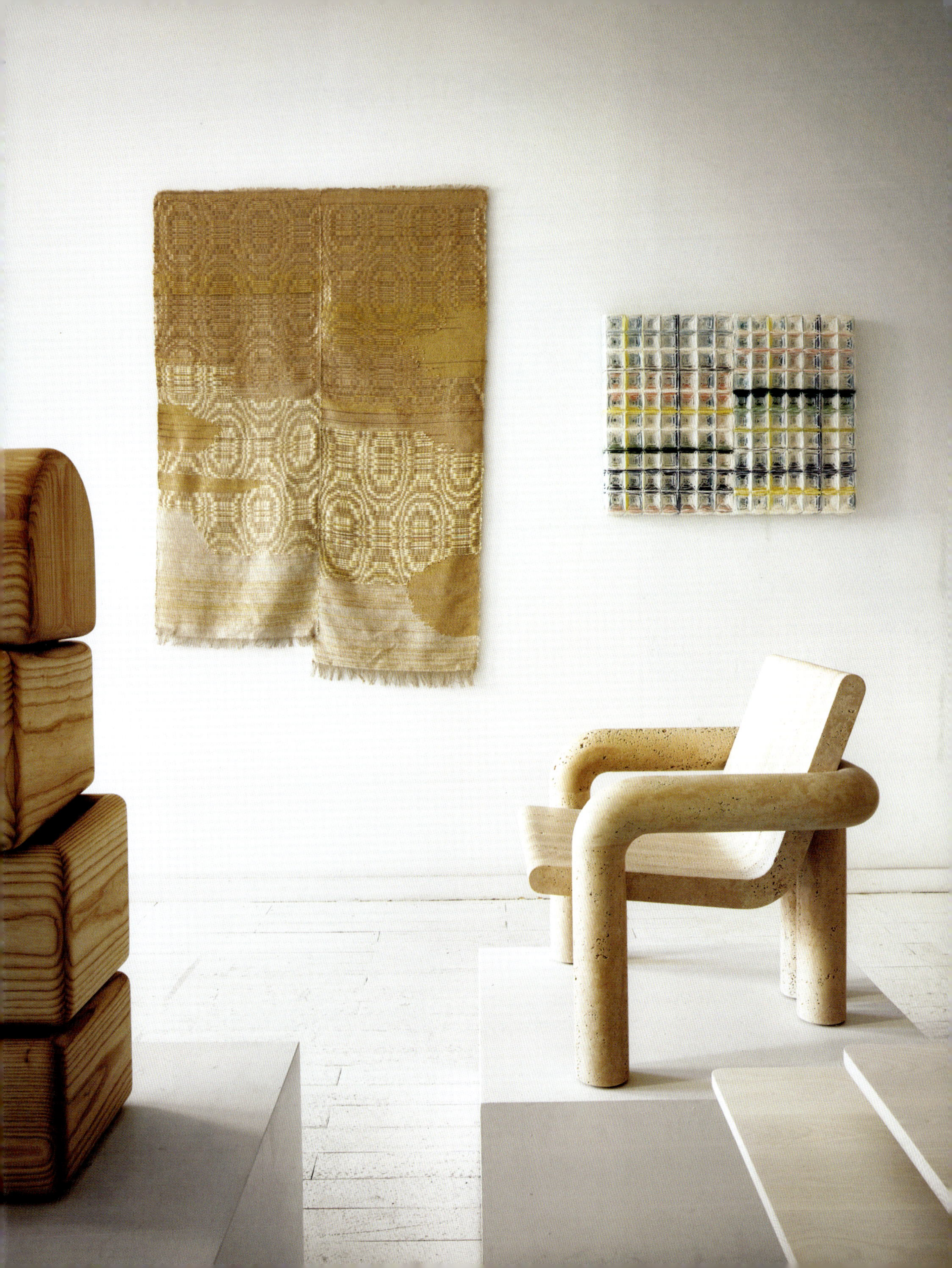

Acknowledgments

Thank you, Drew, for dreaming my dreams with me and believing fiercely in their inevitability. And Juno, you are everything good, whoever you choose to become.

This book would not have been possible without the following people, who have walked with me to where I stand today, and who I love.

Thank you to:

My family
Drew, Juno, Ma, Ba, Jason (for unwavering and early belief), Jasper (for quiet comprehension), Jenna (for accepting our quirks), Jordan, Mia, Kira, Jaden, Harrison.

My team
Madeleine, Brooke (for creative mind meld), Dan, Grace, Mutsumi (my hair), Mayumi (also my hair), Nastassja Isabelle and Tameka (for reviving the 10 to win), Annie, Kimberley, Clare.

My support
Ali Morris, Neil Davies, Alex Parsons Stevens, Michael Chen, Andy Beck, Max Worrell, Jejon Yeung, Lanette Rizzo, Ryden Rizzo, Katy McNally, Freyja McNally-Gnatek, Thora McNally-Gnatek, Rory Panagotopulos, Judy Panagotopulos, Elizabeth Viano, Allyson Rees, Tommy Wenzlau, Mallory Melander Wenzlau, Kai-wei Hsu, Hiroko Takeda, David Hellman, Meg Callahan, James Tanaka, Seth Cohen, Aaron Goldberg, Clay Stuart, Harriet Stuart, Valli Harrison, Al Harrison, Ingemar Hagen-Keith, Emily Rae Pellerin, Ryan Weldon, Robert Higa, Mike Jansson, Katie Jansson, Jen Krichels, Ayumi Sugiyama, Karen Brooking, Tommy Roberts, Bennett Friedman, David Iwaszkiewicz, Bec Brittain, Paolo Ferrari, Courtney Lauderdale, Morgan Spaulding, Brian Kraft, Katrina Vonnegut, Ben Erickson, Ginger Gordon, Alexis Tingey, Thomas Yang, Maggie Pei, Stephanie Betesh, Alara Alkan, Syrette Lew, Nate Scheibe, Rachel Griffin, Anna Aristova, Roza Gazarian, Sarah Sherman Samuel, James Minola, Chelsea Minola.

And thank you to my editor, Shawna Mullen, for finding me in the din of voices and believing that I could write this book. The opportunity to take the sentiments and images that existed in my head and place them onto these pages has been a dream come true.

About the Author

Jean Lin is a New York City–based design entrepreneur and the founder of the downtown design gallery and studio Colony. Trained as a fashion designer, she has professional experience as a fashion designer, an interior designer, editor, writer, trend forecaster, educator, and curator. She has served as part-time faculty at her alma mater, Parsons School of Design, and as a guest lecturer and critic at Rhode Island School of Design, Pratt Institute, Massachusetts College of Art and Design, and Tama Art University in Tokyo.

The daughter of Taiwanese immigrants, Jean came of age in the eighties and nineties in a middle-class Asian household in Massachusetts suburbia. Design, style, and aesthetics were not a consideration in her home, while family, integrity, and hard work were. After a few slightly rebellious years, Jean finally came to understand the power and merit of the latter. Only after she embraced her heritage of values has Jean been able to fully explore who she truly is and what she has to offer the world: finding and sharing the substance behind beauty beyond what is most readily prescribed.

jeanlin.com
goodcolony.com

Contributors

Thank you endlessly to all the people and organizations who contributed to the making of this book.

Dania Ahmad, Goodword PR, *goodwordpr.com*

Allied Maker, *alliedmaker.com*

A Space, *aspacestudio.com*

Elodie Blanchard, *elodieblanchard.com*

Jonathan Boyd, Boyd & Allister, *boydandallister.com*

Brent Buck, Brent Buck Architects, *brentbuckarchitects.com*

Meg Callahan, M. Callahan Studio, *megcallahan.com*

Michael K Chen, MKCA, *mkca.com*

Jennifer Choi and Bruno del Ama

Nina Cho, *ninacho.com*

Phillip Collins, Good Black Art, *goodblackart.com*

Carly Cushnie, *carlycushnie.com*

Deborah Czeresko, *deborahczeresko.com*

DeMuro Das, *demurodas.com*

Erickson Aesthetics, *ericksonaesthetics.com*

Azar Fattahi, Lia McNairy, and LALA Reimagined, *lalareimagined.com*

Studio Paolo Ferrari, *paoloferrari.com*

Christine Gachot, Gachot Studios, *gachotstudios.com*

Evan Geisler, Geisler Projects, *geislerprojects.com*

Aleishall Girard Maxon, Girard Studio, *aleishallgirardmaxon.com*, *girardstudio.com*

Robert Highsmith, Workstead, *workstead.com*

Kai-wei Hsu, KWH Furniture, *kwhfurniture.com*

J. Jih, Studio J. Jih, *j.jih.studio*

Enis Karavil, SANAYI313, *sanayi313.com*

Anna Karlin, Anna Karlin Studio, *annakarlin.com*

Cheryl Katz and Jeffrey Katz, C&J Katz Studio, *candjkatz.com*

Kathy Lewis and Jess Hinshaw, Shapeless Studio, *shapelessstudio.com*

Leyden Lewis, Leyden Lewis Design Studio, *leydenlewis.com*

Brett Littman, The Noguchi Museum, *noguchi.org*

Chelsea Minola and James Minola, Grain Design, *graindesign.com*

Mira Nakashima, George Nakashima Woodworkers, *nakashimawoodworkers.com*

Kwame Onwuachi, Tatiana, *tatiananyc.com*

Duy Pham and Michael Brown, Speaklow, *speaklownyc.com*

Allyson Rees and Julius Metoyer III

Benjamin Reynaert, Benjamin Reynaert Creative Co, *aspoonfullofbenjamin.com*

Adam Rolston, INC Architecture and Design, *inc.nyc*

Lauren Sands, LES Collection, *lescollection.com*

Maya Schindler, Maya Schindler Studio, *mayaschindlerstudio.com*

Stephanie H. Shih, *stephaniehshih.com*
Shiprock Santa Fe, *shiprocksantafe.com*

Beth Diana Smith, Beth Diana Smith Interior Design, *bethdianasmith.com*

Preeti Sriratana, Modellus Novus, *mndpc.com*

Drew Straus and Rachel Bullock, LAUN Studio, *launlosangeles.com*

Stephen Szczepanek, Sri Threads, *srithreads.com*

Hiroko Takeda, *hirokotakeda.com*

Carlos Runcie Tanaka, *carlosruncietanaka.com*

James Tanaka and Dan Shaw

Marie Trohman, Proem Studio, *proem.studio*

Nathan Ursch, Breuckelen Berber, *breuckelenberber.com*

Ghislaine Viñas, *ghislainevinas.com*

David P. Wedel, Davin Wedel, Global Protection, *globalprotection.com*

Max Worrell and Jejon Yeung, Worrell Yeung, *worrellyeung.com*

For more information on individual works pictured in this book, please contact *info@goodcolony.com*

PHOTOGRAPHY CREDITS

Photographs not listed below by Brooke Holm
Styling and creative direction by Jean Lin
Production Coordinator: Dan Shaw

Pages 16, 56, 86, 140, 168:
Author portraits by Winnie Au
Author portraits' styling by Diana Tsui
Author hair by Mayumi Maeda
Author makeup by Flora Kamimoto

Cover art by Paul Inglis / Turn Gallery

Additional photography credits:
Pages 2–3, 7, 10: photography by Alan Tansey
Page 17: photography by Charlie Schuck
Pages 34, 37, 39: photography by Ben Blood
Pages 40, 203: photography by David Mitchell
Page 53: photograph of George Nakashima courtesy of Nakashima Woodworkers
Pages 57, 188: photography by Eric Petschek
Page 80: photography depicted © John Baldessari 1973.
Courtesy Estate of John Baldessari © 2024
Courtesy John Baldessari Family Foundation
Courtesy Spruth Magers
Page 110: photography by Robin Stein
Page 110: photography by Rinne Allen
Page 110: photography courtesy of Meg Callahan
Page 111: photography by Rachael Larkin
Page 133, image 3: photography by Joshua McHugh
Page 151: photography by Mel Yates
Pages 180, 187: photography courtesy of Girard Studio
Page 191: photography courtesy of James Tanaka

Editor: Shawna Mullen
Designer: Sebit Min
Managing Editors: Mary O'Mara and Annalea Manalili
Production Manager: Kathleen Gaffney

Library of Congress Control Number: 20239466465

ISBN: 978-1-4197-7011-1
eISBN: 979-8-88707-117-6

Text copyright © 2024 Jean Lin

Cover © 2024 Abrams

Published in 2024 by Abrams, an imprint of ABRAMS. All rights reserved. No portion of this book may be reproduced, stored in a retrieval system, or transmitted in any form or by any means, mechanical, electronic, photocopying, recording, or otherwise, without written permission from the publisher.

Printed and bound in China
10 9 8 7 6 5 4 3 2 1

Abrams books are available at special discounts when purchased in quantity for premiums and promotions as well as fundraising or educational use. Special editions can also be created to specification. For details, contact specialsales@abramsbooks.com or the address below.

Abrams® is a registered trademark of Harry N. Abrams, Inc.

ABRAMS The Art of Books
abramsbooks.com